PRAISE FOR *RIGHT FROM THE START*

"Children who have autism are not born with a parent's manual to explain their unusual behaviors and abilities. However, *Right from the Start* provides an insight into why the child is different and how to help them regulate emotions, acquire social and play skills, and accommodate intense sensory experiences. This is the manual that parents need."—**Tony Attwood, PhD, psychologist and author of** *The Complete Guide to Asperger's Syndrome*

"This book is an intimate look at the real-life challenges for families of young children with autism. It's filled with very practical strategies on how to manage their behaviors. A must-read for parents, teachers, and caregivers of children who struggle with emotional self-regulation."—**Mary E. Bove, MD, Children's Hospital of Philadelphia, CHOP Care Network, Delaware County**

"Coping with sensory issues is often a huge challenge for children with autism. This wise book written by a parent and a behavioral specialist consultant offers excellent sensory-motor suggestions to help children become more self-regulated and 'in sync.'"—**Carol Stock Kranowitz, MA, author of** *The Out-of-Sync Child*

"Parents of non-neurotypical children need to know they are not alone. This user-friendly book helps to meet that need. It also provides a myriad of ideas that parents and preschool teachers can use to help children regulate their emotions and behavior, develop key social skills, and manage sensory issues. The many real-life, compelling examples will stimulate parents' and teachers' own creative thinking about how to help their kids in ways consistent with current best practices."—**Susan S. Woodhouse, PhD, psychologist and associate professor of counseling psychology, Lehigh University**

"*Right from the Start* is an excellent resource full of specific strategies and written with a positive perspective. Any parent, teacher, or professional looking for guidance will find this book helpful, giving them hope and specific tools for moving forward with the challenges of raising or working with an autistic child."—**Robin Holcomb, MS, programs director, National Alliance on Mental Illness–Utah**

RIGHT FROM THE START

RIGHT FROM THE START

A Practical Guide for Helping Young Children with Autism

KARIN DONAHUE
KATE CRASSONS

ROWMAN & LITTLEFIELD
Lanham • Boulder • New York • London

Published by Rowman & Littlefield
An imprint of The Rowman & Littlefield Publishing Group, Inc.
4501 Forbes Boulevard, Suite 200, Lanham, Maryland 20706
www.rowman.com

6 Tinworth Street, London, SE11 5AL, United Kingdom

British Library Cataloguing in Publication Information Available

Library of Congress Control Number: 2019949305

∞™ The paper used in this publication meets the minimum requirements of
American National Standard for Information Sciences—Permanence of Paper
for Printed Library Materials, ANSI/NISO Z39.48-1992.

To my mother, Elsa Ramsden, my inspiration,
and to my children, Julia and Justin, the joys of my life.—Karin Donahue

To my mom, Gloria Crassons, whose life work has shown me the
importance of early childhood education. And to my children,
Henry and Reed. These boys have taught me how to love with
a depth I never knew was possible, and they've shown me new
ways of seeing the world.—Kate Crassons

CONTENTS

PREFACE

We decided to collaborate on this book after recognizing from first-hand experience that parents, teachers, and administrators need practical resources to help autistic children be successful. We met when Karin, a behavioral specialist consultant, began working with Kate and her husband to support their son, Henry. At age five Henry was diagnosed with mild autism or what would have been called Asperger's syndrome before that diagnosis was replaced by the broader category of autism spectrum disorder. As Karin helped to put various strategies into place at home and at school, Henry's behavior dramatically improved and his sense of self-worth increased.

Henry was able to make progress when everyone in his life, including family members, teachers, and school administrators, came to realize two key things. First, as a child with autism, Henry has unique needs, and his biggest challenges stem from his neurological difference, not from willfulness or bad choices made on his part. Second, it is not especially difficult to accommodate the needs of children like Henry at home and in a mainstream day care center or preschool, which is most often the educational setting for children on the milder end of the autism spectrum who don't qualify for early intervention or other special programs.

It is vital to broadcast these lessons to parents and educators as rates of autism and other neurodevelopmental conditions continue to rise. The latest statistics from the Centers for Disease Control and Prevention (CDC) show that one in fifty-nine children—and one in thirty-seven boys—has autism, a marked increase from one in sixty-eight children in 2012. Rates of attention deficit hyperactivity disorder (ADHD) are even higher as 9.4 percent of children were diagnosed with the disorder in 2016. As this data suggests, neurodiverse or "atypical" children are, in fact, becoming more typical. And, in school or day care settings, these children are among the population of students who are most vulnerable to the ineffective disciplinary measures all too frequently imposed in the earliest years of learning.

Preschoolers are expelled more often than elementary, middle, or high school students—three times more often, to be exact (Gilliam, 2005). When it comes to children with autism and other neurodevelopmental conditions, rates of expulsion are likely to be even higher, especially since school-age children with disabilities are suspended or expelled at twice the rate of their nondisabled peers (Civil Rights Data Collection, 2013–2014). Given this troubling reality, it is not surprising that many autistic children get off to a rocky start when they begin their first ventures into day care or preschool. In some cases, children with autism might end up attending a number of different programs searching for the right fit, which never materializes. In other cases, families might give up on early schooling altogether, scrambling to find ways to care for children at home.

> **Autistic children are among the population of students who are most vulnerable to the ineffective disciplinary measures all too frequently imposed during the earliest years of learning.**

But no child's early life should begin with a sense of chaos and failure—an idea that is at the heart of this book. We know that autistic children can be successful at home and in early learning environments when we put the right supports in place.

Combining professional expertise with a parent's perspective, we offer real-world guidance so that autistic children can flourish in their preschool years. The strategies we provide to parents and educators are practical, evidence based, and easy to use. Though they address a range of topics, the techniques we discuss cohere in helping children develop the foundational skill of self-regulation, a term that refers to our ability to cope with feelings and reactions. Many current approaches to autism and education emphasize changing children's behavior on the surface or gaining their compliance, but this book is grounded in a different idea: parents and teachers should help autistic children develop skills of self-regulation. If we give children the tools to recognize, assess, and moderate their feelings, we will set them on a path to success, enabling them to thrive from the first moment they set foot in a classroom.

Please see this book's companion website:
www.rightfromthestartautismguide.com.

ACKNOWLEDGMENTS

We are grateful for all the support that made it possible for us to write this book: Northampton Community College and the College of Arts and Sciences at Lehigh University generously provided funding that enabled us to conduct the collaborative research that was necessary for this project. We especially extend our thanks to the chair of Lehigh's English department, Professor Dawn Keetley, for supporting and facilitating our cross-institutional work.

We also thank our colleagues and friends who read parts of the manuscript and offered both encouragement and invaluable feedback: David Aers and Christine Derham, Judith Bennett, Beth Dolan, Cara Hersh, and Julie Paulson.

We are extremely appreciative of our editor, Sarah Jubar, and the staff at Rowman & Littlefield for their enthusiasm and attentiveness throughout the publication process.

Finally, we'd like to thank our families.

Kate is grateful to her husband, David Mayer, for his expert editorial assistance and for holding down the fort when she needed time to write. Thank you for your love and for always making me laugh. I'd also like to thank Mary Snyder, Ann Crassons, and Gloria and Norman Crassons for their unflagging support.

Karin would like to express gratitude to her family: her husband, Steve, for his steadfast love and support, and her children, Julia and Justin, for cheering her on. A special thanks also goes to her father, William Ramsden, for his love and encouragement.

INTRODUCTION

An Exceptional Child, an Unexceptional Story:
A Parent's Perspective on the Preschool Years

> As individual parents and as a community . . . our job is not
> to make a particular kind of child but to provide a protected
> space of love, safety and stability in which children of many
> unpredictable kinds can flourish.
>
> —Alison Gopnik, *The Gardener and the Carpenter*

At only six years old, my son Henry could articulate all too clearly that he felt stuck and that he felt worthless. One day as he dissolved into tears, he began to ask a series of questions that no parent would ever want to hear: "Why do I keep getting angry all the time? Why can't I control myself? I keep trying to stay in control, but I keep losing control." As Henry became more upset, his self-reflections became more introspective and more difficult to bear: "Why did God make me this way? I am a bad and dangerous kid. I want to go back to being a baby because I didn't hurt people then. I don't want to be alive anymore."

It should go without saying that it was incredibly painful to hear my young child speak about himself in this way, to hear him suggest that the world would be a better place without him. It was also nearly as painful to recognize that Henry's remarkable capacity for insight allowed him to see only the depth of the problems he was having and not any potential solutions or ways to move forward.

Henry articulated these troubling self-reflections only months after being diagnosed with autism. Even though Henry looks like a typical child, his neurological system did not develop typically. As a result, Henry struggles to master skills that come much more readily to neurotypical children. He has difficulty not only with physical coordination and fine motor tasks, but also with social interaction and managing his emotions. The early years of Henry's life were especially difficult because he persistently struggled with controlling his impulses and behavior. Though Henry was aware of what others expected from him, he was also painfully conscious of his inability to meet those expectations. As a result, he often felt like a failure and expressed a sense of despair that no one would wish upon any child.

In spite of these difficulties, it was also obvious from a very early age that Henry was a smart, funny, and kind boy with an excellent memory and a penchant for asking deep, philosophical questions. Yet he frequently became overwhelmed by the intense feelings that were sparked by his over-reactive nervous system. In this sense he struggled most profoundly with self-regulation, the ability to moderate one's emotions and reactions.

Henry angered easily, experienced frustration quickly, and sometimes acted aggressively even though he knew such behavior was wrong and even though he strove mightily to maintain self-control. For many children like Henry who fall at the milder end of the spectrum, the most obvious manifestation of autism is difficulty with self-regulation. Yet few people recognize how this challenge is linked to autism and the emotional struggles it entails.

This lack of understanding is something that my husband and I felt acutely as we searched to find an appropriate day care center or preschool setting for our son. As two working parents with no family members close by, we first enrolled Henry in day care when he was six months old. Although he did well initially, he began to demonstrate behaviors like biting and hitting at the age of two, right around the time his younger brother was born. In the months that followed, this behavior persisted, and in an effort to ameliorate the problems and help Henry thrive, we moved him to a second day care center when he was almost three.

Although things went better in this new environment, Henry's behavioral issues did not resolve. Over the next couple of years, as we pursued evaluations and tried to discover the root of our son's issues, he completed a year of prekindergarten at a private school. The following year he went to public school for morning kindergarten, and he attended an afternoon program at a local preschool that was designed to supplement the half-day kindergarten classes offered by our school district.

In some of these instances my husband and I made the choice to move Henry to a different school setting; in other instances that choice was made for us. But the point is that we never planned to make so many changes in our son's early life, nor did we want him to have to undergo so many transitions. The difficulties in these early years meant that Henry, a child who needed consistency and routine, ended up attending four different preschools or day care centers all before the age of six.

None of these educational environments, moreover, was able to serve fully Henry's distinctive needs as a child who would eventually be diagnosed with autism. We moved Henry through a series of different day care centers and preschools in a sense of desperation because we did not know what else to do. Even though his behavioral issues remained apparent, he never qualified for early intervention programs or special education classes. This was true even after Henry received a diagnosis of autism.

Henry's chaotic experience in a range of early learning environments is a story worth telling because it entails important lessons for other parents and teachers who care for and work with young children on the autism spectrum. Given that diagnostic rates of autism and other neurodevelopmental conditions are on the rise, there will continue to be many other children like Henry out there in the world. And given that there are few institutional supports for young children on the higher functioning end of the spectrum, there will continue to be many other teachers and parents struggling to understand why some children do not respond to the methods that work well for others.

In writing this book, we decided to begin with an account of Henry's preschool years to put a human face on children who experience behavioral challenges. These are children who are doing the best they can with the emotional resources they have (Greene, 2014b). In beginning with Henry's story, we also seek to show that conventional approaches to education and behavior management do not always work for autistic children who so often struggle with self-regulation.

The unfortunate reality for Henry is that he never got to be part of an early education environment in which he could truly flourish. We do not want other children to have the same experience, and we believe that all kids deserve the chance to feel successful. This goal is especially important when it comes to a child's educational experiences. Children with autism and other needs stand to benefit most from the structure and opportunities for socialization that a preschool or day care setting can provide. We hope that parents and teachers can learn from Henry's difficult journey to help all children be successful in their early years of life. If the lessons from Henry's preschool years can help keep any other young child from feeling worthless, from feeling like the world would be a better place without him, then it is worth telling this story.

AUTISM CAN BE AN ILLUSORY DIAGNOSIS

Many young children with autism aren't eligible for special needs programming because they are "high functioning" and do not necessarily look all that different from typical kids. But their needs *are* different due to a neurological disorder that does not always manifest itself in obvious ways. If these children are to be successful at home and in an early learning environment, it's important that parents and teachers know what autism looks like, especially in its more illusory high-functioning forms.

These children need to be recognized as having special needs that merit some forms of accommodation. This is especially true when the characteristics of children with high-functioning autism do not conform to more widespread conceptions of autistic people who are frequently imagined as being nonverbal and thoroughly self-engaged or as possessing savant-like abilities along with obvious forms of disability.

In Henry's case, he entered the world as a healthy, if colicky, infant who went on to reach all the major developmental milestones on time. He smiled before he was three months old; he babbled profusely as a young baby; he reached for objects at the right stage, and so forth. As parents, my husband and I did not have any concerns that Henry was not developing typically. He spoke his first word very early, at six months, and by the time he was eighteen months old, Henry was speaking in full, articulate sentences. For example, months before he turned two, he declared, "I would like a strawberry ice cream cake for my birthday party in December, please." Henry was an obviously intelligent child who loved books and who could "read" on his own by reciting many of his favorite stories word for word as he turned the pages and looked at the pictures.

It was not until age two that Henry started exhibiting behavior that especially became a problem at day care. My husband and I initially thought that Henry had a particularly bad case of the "the terrible twos," and we noticed that he became angry and frustrated easily. For example, he might attempt to hit or bite if we tried to help him with something he was struggling with or if we put him in time-out. But because Henry was also a playful and loving boy much of the time, we thought that our son was just a particularly spirited child. Plus, we had recently had a second baby who was born with a congenital birth defect, and we were all going through a period of adjustment.

Yet Henry's difficult behavior did not abate after he turned three and after he gradually adjusted to having a baby brother. It was during this time that we moved Henry to a second day care center, but in this setting, he also sometimes attempted to push or hit other children and the day care staff. At this point we had Henry evaluated for the first time at age three. The evaluation turned up nothing beyond a slight fine motor delay, and we addressed that issue by enrolling Henry in occupational therapy. Months later, after being on a long waiting list, we followed through with a second evaluation, this time performed by a developmental pediatrician. She, too, determined that nothing was awry with Henry developmentally. She remarked on his intelligence and his good vocabulary, and she sent us home with some handouts on tantrums.

Yet as Henry grew from a three-year-old into a four-year-old, the behavioral problems persisted even though we employed strategies from the numerous parenting books we read, sought the help of a child psychologist, set limits at home, and imposed consequences for unacceptable behavior. Although Henry eventually underwent two more rounds of evaluations with doctors and psychologists, he did not receive a diagnosis of any kind until he was evaluated for a fourth time, at age five, when the Autism Diagnostic Observation Schedule (the ADOS test) confirmed that he had autism.

This diagnosis was initially surprising, given that other experts had repeatedly ruled out autism as a possible cause of Henry's behavioral difficulties. My husband and I also naively had assumed that autism applied only to children who were not able to speak and who engaged in obviously stimulating behaviors such as hand flapping. But we learned that Henry's form of autism, which is more akin to the old Asperger's diagnosis, looks very different from the kinds of autism with which we were vaguely familiar. We also learned that children on the milder end of the spectrum tend to be diagnosed later than other children with autism, usually between the ages of five and eight.

This provided some clarity into what was happening with our child, and it also made Henry eligible for behavioral therapy services available through a state-funded program. Even with an autism diagnosis, however, it bears repeating that in terms of his early education, Henry did *not* meet the criteria for early intervention programs or autism support classes. The only option for him throughout his early years was to attend a day care or preschool designed with neurotypical children in mind. Many other children with high-functioning autism find themselves in similar positions, and it's for this reason that parents and teachers alike must come to understand that the needs of children with high-functioning autism are different, even if the children themselves look like typical kids on the surface.

CHALLENGING BEHAVIOR IS NOT THE CORE PROBLEM

Recognizing the distinctive needs of children with autism is the first step in understanding the causes of their more challenging behavior. The greatest source of difficulty for everyone during Henry's preschool years was obviously his aggressive behavior. Such behavior was a challenge for teachers who understandably wanted everyone in the classroom to feel safe and to abide by the rules. It was a challenge for us as parents seeking to raise a child who treated others with kindness and respect. And it was a challenge for Henry himself as a child who clearly knew right from wrong and who wanted to do well.

But his ability to make good choices and to control his impulses seemed to get hijacked by moments of intense emotions when frustration or anger quickly overwhelmed him. Everyone involved in Henry's early education was troubled and perplexed by this problem. His teachers saw a child with a kind heart, a child they praised for having excellent manners and empathy for other kids. Yet Henry could very quickly lash out at his peers, or, as was more often the case, at a teacher or authority figure who might have reprimanded him or made him feel intimidated. As his parents, my husband and I knew Henry to be a fundamentally loving and affectionate child, and we provided our sons with a stable home and clear rules about what behavior was and was not acceptable in our family.

Without any obvious causes for Henry's difficult behavior, however, it became all too easy for everyone—us included—to blame the problems on our parenting. For example, the director of Henry's first day care speculated that we were leaving Henry there too long while I was home on maternity leave with our newborn. My husband and I worried that this might be true, but we also knew that we had valid reasons for keeping Henry's schedule consistent in a familiar environment, especially as I was occupied with taking our new baby to a near-constant stream of doctors' appointments in preparation for an upcoming surgery.

The director of Henry's second day care center suggested that his behavioral problems might resolve if we were firmer disciplinarians at home. We worried that this might be true, but we also knew that we were holding firm on consequences for unacceptable conduct. However, this strategy never seemed to prevent future occurrences of a problem behavior despite spending many hours doing things like forcibly returning Henry to his time-out spot until he sat there for a full five minutes. Additionally, we watched as our younger son, who never had any behavioral issues, did well in the same day care environment that proved to be so challenging for

Henry. If the problem was simply a matter of lax discipline at home, why would only one of our children have difficulties with behavior, while the other had none?

My husband and I found that commonplace explanations for Henry's behavior became more frequent and less convincing over time. Once we discovered that Henry had autism and once we began to learn more about the condition, we started to see his challenging behavior in a different light. What looked like willful aggression was actually behavior stemming from his hyperreactive and immature neurological system.

In some cases, for example, he might have pushed another child not because he was trying to hurt a peer, but because he was seeking sensory input that his body craved. At other times, he might have been trying to escape some sensation that felt excruciating to him, even though others would hardly notice anything bothersome. A particular smell or texture might have overwhelmed his nervous system; bright lights, loud noises, or a crowded room might put him over the edge at a certain moment, especially if he was tired or hungry.

> **What looked like willful aggression was actually behavior stemming from a hyperreactive and immature neurological system.**

As both of my children grew older, it became clearer that Henry perceived the world and its sensations in a way that was different from his neurotypical brother. Cutting nails was a breeze for one of my sons, while for the other one it seemed like a form of torture. For one child, putting on socks and shoes was a simple part of the morning routine; for the other child it might take fifteen tries and a tremendous amount of angst to get the seams positioned just right so as not to bother him. One child could do a forward roll and pedal his tricycle the first time he tried; the other child, who almost always kept his body upright, simply couldn't make himself flip over despite trying with mounting frustration fifty consecutive times, nor could he get the hang of pedaling without weeks of practice and, again, much frustration.

Once we knew what to look for, my husband and I could see in obvious ways that Henry was just wired differently than his brother and other neurotypical kids. We came to realize that much of his challenging behavior was a maladaptive strategy for managing overwhelming sensations or for releasing frustration that often stemmed from his motor and sensory difficulties.

If we had been able to identify at least some of the underlying causes for Henry's defensive and reactive behavior sooner, we could have worked with Henry's teachers to help prevent it in the first place. No one, of course, wants to be on the receiving end of anger or aggression, and it's tempting to meet such behavior with an equally forceful response.

For example, it's easy to imagine how parents or teachers might raise their voices to a child who is acting out, stridently reprimanding him for his poor choices and possibly crowding into his personal space. There were certainly moments when we responded in this way as parents. But we saw Henry's most challenging behavior decline when we began to view it as a misguided form of communication, a desperate means of conveying some kind of need during a moment when he couldn't access emotional language.

It is possible to send the clear message that some types of behavior are not acceptable while also attempting to identify the underlying reason for such behavior. If we can begin to think of difficult behavior as a symptom of a larger problem and not as the problem in and of itself, then we can begin to address the challenging behavior more effectively by anticipating triggers and building skills the child may lack.

FLEXIBILITY IS A MODE OF TEACHING

If teachers and parents can become detectives seeking to identify the causes of problem behavior, then it's important to take the next step of work-ing with the child to help eliminate that behavior, a process that happens gradually. This means that the child should learn to manage his emotional responses *and* that the adults in his life should also adjust their own behav-iors and expectations to help him reach that goal.

Early on during times when Henry's difficult behavioral episodes flared up, my husband and I would find ourselves being sucked into a state of ex-treme anxiety fueled in large part by other people's highly reactive responses to our son's behavior. At times, it felt like school personnel saw Henry as a willfully defiant child; conversations with administrators usually led to the declaration—either implicitly or explicitly—that their school had a "zero tolerance" policy on aggressive behavior or that Henry would need to be put on some kind of "probationary enrollment."

Though I do not seek to diminish the very real concerns that a child's challenging behavior can pose to the other people in a school environment, my husband and I found that this hard-line approach seemed only to exacer-bate the very problems it was meant to thwart. For example, on one occasion after Henry hit a teacher at day care, the director told us that our three-year-old posed a "danger" (her word) to her staff. Needless to say, we found this assertion to be distressing, and we felt perplexed imagining the possibility that our little boy posed an actual threat to fully grown adults while also wondering about the validity of the director's perspective. Such statements ultimately served little purpose beyond making us feel more anxious about Henry's behavior. That anxiety, in turn, trickled down to him as we consciously and subconsciously put more pressure on him to try harder, to make better choices, to earn bigger prizes, to face more severe consequences, and to stop, above and beyond all else, failing at day care or preschool so that he would not be kicked out. We wanted Henry to become more flexible and to learn self-soothing skills; yet virtually all the adults in Henry's life—us included—were modeling rigid and reactive responses to a problem.

Although my husband and I agreed that there should be consequences for extreme behavior, we also gradually recognized that the rigidity and reactiveness of school personnel increased the anxiety of everyone in our family, and that anxiety only made it harder for Henry to be successful. On one occasion after Henry had been sent home from preschool for hitting a teacher, he fell into a total state of despair. He was desperate to get back to school; he was distraught at our disappointment; he was worried that our family would run out of money because one of us had to leave work to pick him up; and he vowed repeatedly to be "a good boy" when he was at school.

In making all of these statements, it was clear that Henry felt an overwhelming sense of remorse, shame, and failure. But none of these feelings or realizations ever made it possible for Henry to control his impulses on future occasions or to make good choices when his nervous system had launched him so swiftly into a fight-or-flight response. So being sent home or being put on probation in preschool could not be effective in making Henry finally shape up, in somehow prompting him to decide that, at last, he would stop being "bad." The reality is that Henry was never bad—he was autistic.

It would have benefitted everyone involved in Henry's education to meet his difficult behavior not with ineffectual disciplinary measures, but with appropriate consequences stemming from the recognition that his escalated behavior was as harmful to him as it was to the adults who were the main target of his anger. Additionally, it would have benefitted everyone involved to recognize that Henry's most intense behaviors were not simply the result of noncompliance, but reactions to stimuli in his environment that his body couldn't handle.

For instance, on one occasion during his kindergarten year, Henry escalated into a meltdown because he refused to wash his hands before lunch. We all knew that Henry had a strong sensory aversion to having wet hands and using paper towels, and we all knew that Henry's behavior also notoriously took a nosedive when he was hungry. In this instance, a meltdown likely could have been avoided if the adults who were present had approached the problem flexibly, doing something as simple as allowing Henry to use one of the hand wipes in his backpack as an alternative to washing his hands. This option would have accommodated his sensory needs while also fulfilling the necessity of having clean hands before lunch. Perhaps most importantly, it would have enabled Henry to eat his lunch right away, thereby keeping his blood sugar steady, a key factor in regulating his behavior.

On this occasion, perhaps Henry's teachers did not consider a viable alternative to washing hands because they thought that he should comply with the rules like all the other kids. It is understandable that teachers and parents alike might worry that taking a flexible approach could undercut their authority and inadvertently reward a child's seemingly inappropriate and demanding behavior. But in working with our son, my husband and I found the opposite to be true. If a child perceives his teachers and parents as people who take his perspective and his concerns seriously, then the child will develop a bond of trust that comes to serve as the foundation of the adult's authority and influence over the child. Leading autism expert Barry Prizant affirms this idea when he says that "autism can be best understood as a disability of trust." People with autism, he notes, have difficulty when it comes to "trusting their body, trusting the world around them, and—most challenging of all—trusting other people" (2015, 73).

Autistic children will flourish only when they recognize that the adults in their life approach them with compassion and take their needs seriously. When parents and teachers address challenging behavior thoughtfully, rather than immediately responding with a forceful demand, autistic children also benefit from having models of people who choose deliberation over impulsive reaction, flexibility over rigidity, and self-possession over seemingly uncontrollable emotion.

SOCIAL AND EMOTIONAL LEARNING IS A PRIORITY

Henry's sharp intellect always has been one of his many strengths, and although my husband and I wanted him to do well academically even as he started preschool, we also realized that the school environment was just as important for teaching him social and emotional lessons. In the earliest years of school or childcare when children can play with toys, spend time on the playground with their peers, and share thoughts with one another during group time, we assumed that social interaction and emotional fluency naturally would emerge as the greatest learning priorities. But especially as Henry entered the elementary school years, my husband and I were surprised by how quickly academics seemed to become the all-consuming focus.

Henry had a busy morning of learning during his year of kindergarten at public school, and we had hoped that his afternoon program would offer him further opportunities for practicing social skills and enjoying some downtime with his peers. But Henry's time in this educational environment proved to be a challenge because we found it difficult to partner with his teachers to develop a shared set of educational goals for our son. This was true even though Henry's most challenging behavior had decreased significantly by this point.

We recognized and appreciated that Henry's teachers wanted to provide him with a solid foundation for going into first grade the following year. Yet in thinking about our son as a five-year-old child with autism, we believed that after a full morning of kindergarten, Henry would benefit most not from additional academic training in the afternoons, but from opportunities to play with other children and practice social skills.

Therefore it was okay with us if he did not complete something like a handwriting exercise because it took him extra time to transition to that activity, a nonpreferred task with which he struggled. It was not that we were unconcerned with Henry's schoolwork; rather we thought that there was an important foundation that needed to be laid before we should start worrying about Henry's performance on things like math tests and literacy assessments. Henry still needed to learn the much more basic lessons—which come effortlessly to most other children—that school is a place where he could make friends and feel supported.

My husband and I found it hard to persuade Henry's teachers that these distinctive goals should be prioritized for him. In meetings with the school staff, the pressure that the teachers felt to prepare students for the academic rigors of future grades was palpable. Our requests that they focus on helping Henry develop social and emotional skills were often met with looks of puzzlement and concern that we were not taking Henry's education seriously. We, of course, wanted Henry to do well in first grade and in the years that followed, but there seemed to be a disconnect between the teachers' short-term goals of helping Henry master basic reading and math skills and our long-term goals of helping him learn to manage his emotions and see his time in school as a positive experience.

Even though we knew that Henry was highly intelligent, we acknowledged the possibility that in focusing on these other objectives, we might, at a later point, need to help him catch up academically, if necessary. But from our perspective, all the phonics lessons and math problems in the world would be useless without his mastery of foundational social and emotional lessons. We were therefore prioritizing skills of self-regulation precisely because we cared so much about the importance of education and because we did not want Henry to be averse to the many years of school still ahead of him. But the pressures to produce academically proficient students, even in first grade, seemed to obscure the inherently logical connection between educational and emotional goals.

THIS STORY IS NOT UNUSUAL OR INEVITABLE

Though Henry's chaotic preschool years attest to the difficulties he faced as a young child, his experience is also indicative of a wider need for mainstream education programs that can offer knowledgeable support of young children with autism. Children like Henry tend to slip through the cracks when it comes to early education. They find themselves unable to succeed in a typical learning environment while, at the same time, they are also deemed ineligible for special education or early intervention programs. From the moment they enter day care or preschool, these children need teachers who, in a combined effort with parents, pursue broad pedagogical goals that include a focus on teaching social skills and strategies for managing strong feelings.

In my experience with Henry, I found that it was not especially hard for him to learn how to read, count, and recognize shapes, but he did need expert help in learning how to be successful in a world that he perceives differently from others. Most importantly, autistic children like Henry need models—inside and outside the classroom—of how to be flexible and maintain self-control. They need the adults in their lives not only to teach explicit lessons about social skills and feelings, but to become the living embodiments of those lessons. Through their own actions, parents and teachers can invite children into a way of being that gradually enables them to cope with frustration, to manage uncomfortable sensations, to communicate difficult feelings through language, and to modulate their emotions in the face of often overwhelming anxiety.

In writing this book, we understand how difficult it might feel for mothers, fathers, and other caretakers to let go of certain parenting conventions even when it's clear they're not effective for some kids. I've learned from firsthand experience how hard it can be to shift the expectations I had of myself and my child, to let go of unproductive techniques I assumed were fail-safe, and to experiment with new strategies that I felt unsure about.

We also understand how daunting it can appear to expect teachers to adapt their traditional modes of instruction to accommodate students with a varied range of abilities. When interacting with autistic children at home or at school, it can certainly feel intimidating to take risks and experiment with different approaches as we seek to win their engagement and teach them effectively. However, we know from experience that it's surprisingly easy to overcome these fears and challenges—especially when parents and teachers work together.

One of the basic tenets of this book is that autistic children should feel successful in their early years of life and see their time in day care, at home, or in preschool as a positive experience that sets the tone for their future years of education. We seek to make this an attainable goal by offering research-based strategies for helping young children with autism at home and school. These strategies make it possible to create supportive environments that can meet the needs of autistic students without generating untenable burdens for teachers and families.

In the first section of this book, we explore the concept of self-regulation and explain why this skill is the foundation of a child's future growth and development. In the rest of the book, we cover four major areas of need for autistic children, highlighting how challenges in different aspects of development all impact a child's ability to self-regulate. We include sections on managing emotions and behavior, developing social skills, engaging in play, and addressing sensory processing issues.

In considering these topics, we explain the root causes of what might look like mere behavior problems, and we offer practical strategies for helping children overcome various skill deficits that, in turn, affect their ability to self-regulate. Designed for easy implementation at home and in any mainstream classroom, these strategies offer benefits not just to children with autism, but to their neurotypical siblings and peers as well. In giving autistic children the tools to deal with the various difficulties they face, we sharpen their skills in specific areas, and we also facilitate their overall capacity for self-regulation, an essential lifelong skill.

Perhaps most importantly, we should remember as parents and teachers that our efforts in supporting autistic children are a worthy investment. Although autism is recognized as a disability, children on the spectrum also possess exceptional abilities that need to be cultivated in the classroom and beyond. I see these abilities and strengths every day in my son. Henry is a child who has a heart of gold; a child who frequently tells my husband, his brother, and me that he will love us forever; a child who will snuggle with us every chance he gets; a child who loves to tell jokes and who makes his brother laugh like no one else can; a child who picks up stray trash so that birds won't eat it and get sick.

He is a child with an inquisitive mind that deserves to be nurtured. He thinks deeply and wants to know exactly where heaven is and why we can't see it; he wonders why God made us if we all have to die. He wants to be a scientist so that he can invent a machine to make everyone's bad memories go away.

He is a child who is good; a child who is full of promise.

I

SELF-REGULATION
The Key to Making It through the Day

We all do our best to self-regulate in different ways. For example, when we are driving at night and feel tired, we try to arouse our senses. We might roll down the window to get some fresh air. We might turn up the radio, or we might stop to get a cup of coffee. We engage in strategies to help stimulate our nervous system.

On other occasions, we engage in strategies to help calm down. For example, if we get upsetting news, we might talk to a friend, ask for help, or think about our options for dealing with the situation. Every day, we use a variety of techniques to self-regulate, to control our feelings and behavior.

> **Self-regulation: the ability to manage one's emotions and behavior.**

We recognize how important it is to manage our emotions because it does not feel good to be out of control.

For children especially, self-regulation is "the key to making it through the day." When a child is self-regulated, he is able to cope with emotional highs and lows, control his reactions, and remain calm. Children on the autism spectrum often have difficulty with self-regulation for a number of reasons. Some of this difficulty arises from the specific skill deficits associated with autism. For example, because autistic children often struggle to understand the perspectives of others, they are likely to feel anxious and confused in social situations. This heightened emotional state can make children feel out of control, leading to inappropriate or impulsive behavior.

The sensory processing issues that come with autism often create similar problems. Because ordinary sensations in the environment can feel overwhelming to autistic children, their discomfort can cause them to become irritated, upset, or uncooperative. These social and sensory challenges frequently lead to the same end point, resulting in a child who loses the capacity to control his emotions and behavior. Self-regulation is a concept that underpins the many facets of autism and the variety of skill deficits it entails.

For children on the spectrum, difficulty with self-regulation is also important as its own psychological issue not necessarily related to social and sensory challenges. Due to their neurological differences, autistic children in general become frustrated, agitated, or thrown off track more readily than their neurotypical peers. They often have difficulty monitoring their reactions and behavior.

Their experience of dysregulation can sometimes be mild, manifesting itself in behavior such as hand flapping, walking in circles, or talking in long monologues. At other times when children are dysregulated, they might refuse to follow directions, cry, or scream. And in extreme cases, a dysregulated child can launch into a fight-or-flight response. As the child's nervous system reacts instinctively to a perceived threat, he might respond to a situation with aggression, or he might attempt to escape the stressful circumstances.

SIGNS OF DYSREGULATION		
• Hand flapping • Walking in circles • Talking in monologues	• Refusing to follow directions • Crying • Screaming	• Experiencing the "fight or flight" sensation • Engaging in aggression • Eloping
Level of Intensity		

At any level of intensity, the experience of feeling dysregulated leads to challenging behavior and interferes with a child's ability to learn and function successfully in a range of environments. It is for these reasons that this book seeks to help children with autism gain the fundamental skill of self-regulation.

We turn now to discuss the importance of this concept and to demonstrate its relevance to the other key aspects of autism addressed in this book. In the chapter that follows, we first make the case for focusing on self-regulation as a foundational skill. Developing a basic philosophy of self-regulation, we explain the reasons why it is ultimately more important to prioritize this skill than to push a child to meet demands in other areas. We then examine why autistic children so often struggle to manage their feelings as a result of differences in brain structure.

1

THE CASE FOR SELF-REGULATION

Matthew, a four-year-old boy on the autism spectrum, arrives at school in the morning, greets his teacher, Mrs. Landry, and heads off to the train table where he and another classmate have fun using their trains to deliver coal. Matthew soon becomes engrossed in trying to make his own train as long as possible, but the train keeps coming apart when he adds too many cars, and he becomes increasingly frustrated. After a few minutes, Mrs. Landry announces that it is circle time, and Matthew transitions to the carpet area with the other children, but he remains focused on the train that he could not build successfully. Squirming and twisting to look back at the train table, Matthew hears repeated reminders from Mrs. Landry to sit still and pay attention.

As circle time ends, Matthew finds that, because it is raining, the class will move into centers immediately instead of following their usual routine and going outside. When Mrs. Landry directs Matthew to the art center, he suddenly exclaims, "I hate art! I'm going back to the train table." Mrs. Landry tells him that they are making a jack-o'-lantern for Halloween and that he will have fun at the art center, but Matthew starts crying and says, "I'm not doing that dumb artwork." Mrs. Landry then firmly reminds him that everyone is expected to go to his assigned center and leads Matthew to his seat at the art table, where he tries to trace and cut out a circle.

Matthew finds it difficult to cut on the curved lines, and he suddenly yells, "I hate this!" and throws his scissors across the table. The scissors graze the arm of a girl sitting near him, who begins to cry. Mrs. Landry then tells Matthew, "We don't throw scissors at people. That is dangerous. We do not hurt our friends. You are going into time-out." Mrs. Landry's stern demeanor makes Matthew more upset, and he thinks he shouldn't have to go to time-out because he didn't mean to hurt his classmate. He tries to run away, but Mrs. Landry intercepts Matthew and brings him back to the time-out area. He refuses to stay put, however, and Mrs. Landry takes Matthew to the school director so that she can deal with him in her office.

How can we make sense of the dramatic deterioration in Matthew's behavior? How does the pleasant and cooperative boy who arrives at school turn into a seemingly noncompliant child who nearly injures a classmate? The answer to this question lies in the concept of self-regulation.

A rested, calm, and non-defensive child is a child who is self-regulated. When he is in this emotional state—that is, when he feels "just right"—a child is able to be successful at home, at school, or in virtually any environment. Lacking the ability to self-regulate, a child can become overwhelmed by the smallest of problems, and his behavior can spiral out of control. This proves to be the case with Matthew, who is able to self-regulate at the beginning of the school day, but whose emotional resources dwindle after a long morning filled with various challenges and unexpected events.

As we turn now to explain the importance of self-regulation and to examine how autism affects this skill, we will revisit Matthew's story intermittently to offer concrete examples of the topics at hand.

RECOGNIZING CHALLENGES

When interacting with autistic children we should always prioritize skills of self-regulation, making accommodations and offering support so that they can maintain self-control or regain self-control after a period of dysregulation. Autistic children have the best chance of flourishing and making developmental gains if they can avoid feeling totally overwhelmed as they go about their day.

Given that autistic children have unique needs that are not always obvious, we must first acknowledge that seemingly ordinary activities can present significant challenges for children on the spectrum. If we consider Matthew in the example above, we can see that a simple art project is much more demanding for him than it is for his neurotypical peers because he has delayed fine motor skills, a common occurrence in autistic children.

When we encourage these children to participate in "fun" activities, we must proceed by recognizing that we are also quite possibly asking them to move out of their comfort zones, a prospect that can provoke anxiety, resistance, and other forms of dysregulation. Our job, therefore, is to help children stretch *within limits*, encouraging them to think more flexibly and to try something that is new or difficult without spiraling into a complete state of dysregulation.

For example, if we want to play a board game with a child at home on a rainy day, but we know that the child often gets angry or gives up because it feels impossible to win, then we can amend the rules or adjust the structure of the game to help the child cope with her frustration. When the spinner lands on "lose a turn," we can take that to mean "spin again." Or we can play a game like Memory, using only half or a quarter of the matching cards. These simple changes go a long way toward helping children enjoy and participate successfully in activities that, for them, are often more challenging than fun. It is therefore essential that we acknowledge the individual perspectives of these children. We must do what we can to help them manage the anxiety that will inevitably arise when we ask them to let go of what is familiar and seek out experiences that will be difficult.

PROMOTING SELF-CONTROL

In the moments when a child shows reluctance or escalating behavior, it can be tempting to assert control and to insist, as a general rule, that he must complete the task or activity at hand. It is not uncommon to hear parents, teachers, and even therapists say things like "We cannot let the child escape demands" or "He must learn to do what he is told, even if he does not like it." We certainly agree that children need to heed adult directives and that they must learn to do things that are hard or uncomfortable. However, pushing a child to comply when he is already showing signs of distress often backfires. This is the case with Matthew, who refuses to go to the art table not because he just wants his own way, but because he struggles to perform tasks such as writing, drawing, and cutting. Knowing that he will not be as successful as his peers even if he tries his best, he feels anxious about the jack-o'-lantern craft, and this anxiety drives his aversion to the task.

Matthew, to his credit, eventually complies with Mrs. Landry's demand to work at the art center, but he undertakes the project at a point in the day when he lacks the resources needed to tolerate the frustration he experiences when engaging in fine motor activities. As Matthew struggles to cut out the jack-o'-lantern, his feelings of incompetence reach their boiling point, and, in this moment, he throws the scissors. Although this reaction is unacceptable and potentially dangerous, it is also a sign that Matthew is not in control of his emotions and actions. Matthew does not throw the scissors in a deliberate attempt to defy his teacher or hurt a peer. Rather, his reaction is driven by impulsivity, low frustration tolerance, and diminished self-esteem.

It is telling that no one in this scenario ends up having control despite Mrs. Landry's initial attempt to assert her authority and reaffirm the rules of the classroom. If we trace the scene's chaotic outcome back to the moment when Matthew resists going to the art table, we can see that his refusal is not, fundamentally, a sign of disobedience that can be effectively managed by doubling down on demands. Rather, we must remember the mantra of influential child psychologist Ross Greene: "Kids do well if they can" (Greene, 2014a). Matthew's resistance is a sign of his own latent awareness that the demands of the jack-o'-lantern craft are greater than the skills he possesses in this particular moment. Matthew lacks the fine motor skills necessary to complete the craft, and he also lacks the emotional resilience required to manage the feelings of frustration and ineptitude that he experiences.

> **"Kids do well if they can."**
> **—Ross Greene**

FOSTERING COOPERATION AND ENGAGEMENT

In working to promote self-control and prioritize self-regulation, we do not undermine the message that it is important for children to follow rules and meet expectations. When we support a child's emotional needs, we actually *increase* the chances that he will show compliance and engagement in the long term. There are a few reasons why this is the case.

First, when a child sees that an adult recognizes his feelings and acknowledges their validity, he moves from a position of defensiveness to one of openness and security even in the wake of experiencing potentially extreme emotions. When we register and honor the legitimacy of a child's feelings about a certain task or set of circumstances, we do not cede our authority as parents and teachers. Trying to see the world from a child's perspective does not somehow signal to him that he can do whatever he wants, whenever he wants. Rather, we bolster our authority as parents, teachers, and role models by showing the child that his perspective matters to us.

If we return to the example of Matthew, we can imagine a different outcome that hinges on Mrs. Landry taking a moment to acknowledge and validate the feelings Matthew expresses when he first refuses to go to the art center. This simple act opens the door to a variety of potential solutions that allow Matthew to stay calm while also enabling Mrs. Landry to maintain her expectations for the classroom.

For example, when Matthew makes his initial protest about going to the art table, Mrs. Landry can reflect his feelings back to him, and she can consider the possible reasons for his resistance. Even if Matthew cannot explain precisely why he wants to avoid the art center, Mrs. Landry can recognize that his rather extreme reaction to a small art project is a sign that he feels overwhelmed. She can then suggest that Matthew take a break or do a calming activity in a quiet corner of the classroom. And she can let him know that he can return to the jack-o'-lantern craft later in the day—perhaps after lunch and rest time, when he feels reenergized. Or, it is possible that once Mrs. Landry validates his feelings, Matthew might become less defensive,

Anxiety is often at the root of challenging behavior and resistance to tasks.

seeing his teacher as a source of support. He might willingly move to the art table where he can work with her in assembling the craft so that he can get the help he needs to be successful.

Each of these possibilities is a win-win scenario for everyone involved, since Matthew is able to stay self-regulated *and* complete his work at the art center. More importantly, as a teacher works with a child in this way to offer support and solve a problem, she lays the foundation for the child's future cooperation and growth. She earns his trust by showing him that his emotional well-being is more important than anything else, including a paper jack-o'-lantern.

Coping Skills and the Capacity to Learn

Promoting self-regulation also paves the way for children to meet the expectations of parents and teachers because in order to complete a task they must be able to think logically, pay attention, and exercise flexibility—skills that can be accessed only when children are calm and in control of their emotions. When a child fulfills a demand, he shows that he understands both what is being asked of him and why he should follow through with the expected action. But many autistic children struggle with this mode of social understanding, especially when they are dysregulated and their capacity for rational thinking is compromised by the powerful feelings that overtake them.

For example, consider Matthew's mental and emotional state when he finally joins his peers at the art table. Before he even attempts the jack-o'-lantern craft, Matthew is already dysregulated. He has experienced frustration and a sense of failure at the train table. He has experienced embarrassment at circle time. He has managed an unexpected change in routine by staying inside all morning. And he has missed out on the cognitive and psychological benefits that come from running around, getting fresh air, and leaving the busy classroom for a change of scenery. Given this accumulation of experiences throughout the morning, we can see that Matthew is not going to be able to access the skills he needs to trace, cut, and successfully create a craft, for these are tasks that require great effort and attention even when he is at his best.

Because self-regulation is essential for accessing higher level cognitive skills, it is also important that we do not discipline autistic children unless they are calm enough to comprehend the reasons for the specific consequences we impose. Conventional forms of discipline often backfire in the face of an autistic child's dysregulation, serving to increase the child's intense emotions and problem behaviors.

Self-regulation promotes learning.

This is precisely what happens in Matthew's case when Mrs. Landry attempts to put him in time-out for throwing the scissors. It is clear that Matthew's behavior needs to be addressed. He must learn that there are consequences for our actions regardless of our motivations. But these consequences should function to help Matthew learn to take a different course of action on future occasions when he finds himself highly frustrated. After all, the goal of discipline is to teach, as suggested by the word's Latin root, *disciplina*, which means teaching, learning, or knowledge. But a child cannot absorb the disciplinary lessons a parent or teacher tries to instill when he is deeply agitated or angry. His chaotic feelings overwhelm everything he does, affecting his powers of comprehension and his ability to talk and interact with others.

We see this problem with Matthew when, immediately after he throws the scissors, he runs away from Mrs. Landry, who attempts to put him in time-out. Matthew tries to avoid this consequence not so much because he wants to evade punishment in general, but because he does not understand why he needs to go to time-out in the first place. Even though he knows the difference between right and wrong, he does not think that he is at fault because he never meant to throw the scissors at the girl sitting across from him. He was not angry with her. In fact, he was not thinking about her at all.

Putting Matthew in time-out when he is in an agitated and defensive mode does not effectively address the more immediate issue—that he cannot see the scissors incident from the girl's point of view and recognize his own culpability. Given Matthew's limitations when it comes to perspective taking and social understanding—areas that are commonly challenging for autistic children—it makes sense to wait to address his problem behavior only after he has calmed down. He needs to be receptive to the important lessons he has yet to learn.

Promoting self-regulation is thus ultimately an essential component of effective discipline. When we consider a child's emotional state and his potential struggles with self-control, we can be thoughtful in setting limits, correcting behavior, and imposing consequences for breaking the rules and engaging in unsafe actions. We need to make sure that any disciplinary measures we put in place adequately address and help remedy the skill deficits that so often underlie problem behavior.

We also need to make sure that children themselves see the link between a consequence and a specific mistake they have made so that they can internalize the relevant lessons and respond to a similar problem in a different way the next time. These are the outcomes we seek when we discipline children, and these outcomes only become possible when we consider a child's emotional state and support his capacity for self-regulation.

> **Discipline is frequently ineffective when a child is dysregulated, and it is likely to exacerbate the problem.**

Our overriding goal as parents and teachers should be to teach autistic children flexibility and coping skills while also creating a learning environment where they can feel safe and calm. When children are in this state, they are most likely to be receptive to ideas, rules, or demands that might otherwise provoke disengagement or resistance. We all want children to make progress, to follow directions, and to try new things, even if these endeavors provoke feelings of anxiety or discomfort. Emphasizing self-regulation makes it possible for children to achieve such goals, as they gradually come to recognize that they are capable of pursuing difficult tasks and learning from their mistakes without falling apart, withdrawing into themselves, or dissolving into sadness or anger.

When a child with autism shows signs of dysregulation, his difficulties do not have to snowball into the kind of extreme reaction that Matthew experiences. By focusing on self-regulation, we can go a long way toward preempting such episodes and helping children like Matthew be more successful in preschool, day care, or at home.

In addition to teaching autistic children coping skills, we can also shape our interactions with them and adjust the environment to offer these children support. However, before delving into the strategies for promoting self-regulation, it is first important to understand why this skill often proves especially difficult for autistic children to master.

2

WHY DO AUTISTIC CHILDREN HAVE DIFFICULTY SELF-REGULATING?

This chapter offers a user friendly overview of recent research on autism to explain how difficulties with self-regulation stem from the neurological differences associated with the condition. It is crucial that parents, teachers, and school administrators understand that the behavior challenges often seen in autistic children have a neurological and biological basis. We must recognize that when an autistic child is struggling, she is not simply making a bad choice or acting out to get attention as we might assume with a neurotypical child. To correctly interpret the behavior of an autistic child—and to effectively address challenging behavior—we must first understand its connection to the child's neurological differences.

NEURAL CONNECTIONS IN THE BRAIN

Autism affects the neural connections in the brain that help to assess problems, modulate reactions, and express emotions (Shannon, 2011). The emotional center of the brain, known as the amygdala, is responsible for the perception and regulation of feelings. In people with autism, neuroimaging of the brain reveals abnormalities of the amygdala (Attwood, 2007).

There is also evidence that the neural connectivity between the amygdala and the prefrontal cortex, or the thinking part of the brain, is weakened in people with autism. This faulty connection makes it difficult for autistic people to assess and articulate their feelings. Because autism also affects the prefrontal cortex itself, children on the spectrum can struggle

Autism is a neurological disorder. The brains of children with autism work differently than the brains of neurotypical children.

with organizational skills, logical thinking, decision making, and planning strategies. These deficits also interfere with the ability to self-regulate (Campbell, 2006). We see evidence of this difficulty when a person with autism gets upset but cannot enact coping strategies such as asking for help, taking a break, or telling someone about the problem.

AUTISM AND THE COMPLEXITY OF EMOTIONS

Many children on the autism spectrum have difficulty identifying their feelings, and they tend to express more basic emotions such as sadness or anger. Though a child may be jealous, embarrassed, frustrated, or confused, his experience of these feelings can get balled up into a single emotion. Often, this single emotion is anger, and autistic children can be quick to express mild feelings of annoyance or irritability in a heated or even explosive way.

A minor issue or event can prompt a strong emotional reaction because, for many children on the autism spectrum, all problems seem big. Once a child becomes upset and angry, the overactive amygdala hijacks the prefrontal cortex. When this happens, the emotional powerhouse of the brain overtakes the child's capacity to engage in rational thought and decision making. In these moments, strong feelings of anger, and possibly even rage, dominate a child's thinking and dictate his behavioral choices (Attwood, 2007).

For example, while sitting in her bedroom and looking at her favorite book, three-year-old Margaret sees that one of the pages is ripped. Even though it's only a small tear that doesn't interfere with the words or the pictures, Margaret immediately becomes distraught, and nothing her parents say can soothe her. While sobbing uncontrollably, she rips the page out of the book and crumples it up because, in her mind, the book has already been ruined forever. As is the case with Margaret, many parents describe their autistic child's anger as a "zero-to-sixty" phenomenon: it seems to escalate quickly and without warning, like a race car accelerating to 60 miles per hour in only a few seconds.

If we return to the example of Matthew from the last chapter, we can see just how quickly his behavior turns when he suddenly throws his scissors across the table. No one—including Matthew himself—has been attuned to the growing sense of frustration he feels throughout the morning. Matthew eventually lashes out in response to a minor problem because he is unable to recognize his need to take a break, ask for help, or engage in another coping strategy. Although there are productive ways for children like Matthew to resolve their feelings of frustration, the amygdala's overactive response interferes with the capacity for rational thought, making it impossible to access the cognitive skills needed for problem solving. As a result, feelings of frustration culminate in an explosion of anger.

AUTISM, LANGUAGE, AND COPING SKILLS

Language is an important tool for regulating our emotions. Think about the last time you were very upset. Chances are you told someone how upset you were, and you probably also used "self-talk," a mental language inside your head, to help work through the experience and to consider possible resolutions to the problem. Preschoolers frequently use language and self-talk to work through challenging situations (Szatmari, 2004).

However, autistic children—including those who are highly verbal—might not use self-talk to problem solve (Attwood, 2007). For example, they may learn and process information more visually, "thinking in pictures" (Grandin, 1995).

Examples of self-talk:

"I remember how to do this."
"I can do this."
"I think I need help."

The ability to self-regulate is also affected when a child has difficulty verbalizing feelings. Due to the weak links in the parts of the brain that process emotions, autistic children struggle to understand their feelings and put them into words. In some cases, children might resort to using "mean" or intimidating words, because they cannot find the right language for expressing the torrent of emotions they feel. They may even be heard threatening to kill someone, or saying things like, "I hate you," because they are at a loss for how to verbalize their emotions appropriately.

Four-year-old Arthur, for example, is getting over strep throat, and he has to take his antibiotic even though he *hates* how it tastes. After dealing with a lot of resistance from Arthur, his mother finally corrals him into a corner of the kitchen and gets him to swallow the medicine. Arthur then feels traumatized and yells, "You are the worstest mom! Stay away from me forever!" It's important to note that these kinds of extreme words usually do not express a child's true feelings or intentions. After all, Arthur's mother knows that he truly loves her, and she's aware that he can't fully understand why he must take the medicine. When we hear autistic children speaking in such harsh language, we need to realize that their words function to convey the sense of desperation that overwhelms their ability to cope. Recall from chapter 1 when Matthew shouts "I hate this" before throwing the scissors.

Unable to use language as a resource for coping with frustration, Matthew verbalizes his strong feelings in a counterproductive way.

SELF-AWARENESS AND SOCIAL UNDERSTANDING IN AUTISTIC CHILDREN

In order to control our emotions and behavior, it is helpful to understand, at least to some extent, how our feelings and actions are connected. Children on the autism spectrum tend to have limited self-awareness and struggle with self-reflection. They often do not register the root causes of their emotions, and it can be hard for them to understand the link between their feelings and behavior. They might also have difficulty seeing how their actions potentially affect other people.

For example, while Brianna, age five, is at home on the weekend drawing with her little brother, she tells him that he's a "bad artist" because his drawing of a tiger "is just a bunch of scribbles" that looks nothing like the animal. Later during the week when she's at day care, Brianna sees a classmate working on a puzzle, and she pushes him out of the way, quickly finishing the puzzle for him. On neither of these occasions, however, does Brianna realize that her words and actions cause others to feel sad and disappointed. From her perspective, she's simply reporting the truth to her brother and solving a puzzle because she sees the answer.

It is important to recognize that this limited awareness has a neurological cause. Research suggests that it might stem from weak connections between the prefrontal cortex, the part of the brain that controls decision making and thinking, and mirror neurons, the part of the brain involved in social interactions. These weaker brain connections might also help explain why autistic children can sometimes seem detached from people and events around them. Though they feel emotions like empathy, they might not show those feelings in an obvious or explicit way (Shannon, 2011).

An autistic child's impaired self-awareness affects his self-concept or his sense of self. It also influences his perception of himself in relation to others. Children on the autism spectrum want to interact and make friends but they often do not know how to accomplish this goal because of limited social skills and social knowledge. Three-year-old Joseph, for example, often walks up to other children, whether at school or in the community, and begins tickling them. He tries to engage with other kids in a fun and friendly way, but his actions feel off-putting to his peers because they find that their personal space has been invaded by someone who hasn't even greeted them or asked if tickling them is okay. Though Joseph isn't yet adept at making friends and initiating social contact, he is nonetheless aware that his peers consistently reject his attempts to engage with them. As a result, Joseph thinks that he is not likeable, which greatly harms his developing self-concept.

Whereas neurotypical children often use social cues and support from peers to help them solve problems and interact successfully with others, autistic children generally have difficulty interpreting social information. They not only have trouble reading body language and facial expressions, but also struggle with what is known as theory of mind—the ability to understand someone else's point of view. Daily interactions can cause autistic children to feel anxiety and confusion because they might not be attuned to the fact that other people have thoughts about them and that others' perspectives are different from their own.

Returning to our example of Matthew from chapter 1, we can see Matthew's challenges with theory of mind when he does not register why his teacher and classmate are so upset after he throws the scissors. For Matthew, his intentions were never to hurt anyone, and that is all he understands. His dysregulation and disruptive behavior increase precisely because he cannot see his actions from another perspective besides his own.

AUTISM AND DIFFERENT SENSORY EXPERIENCES

When autistic children take information in through their senses, they do not perceive the world in the same way as their neurotypical peers. Children on the autism spectrum might sometimes experience sensations in a heightened or more detailed manner. For example, bright light, loud sounds, and the feeling of clothing tags against the skin can be very irritating. At other times they might feel things with lessened intensity, like having a high tolerance for pain (Nason, 2014).

A child's ability to self-regulate is affected greatly when his nervous system is easily over- or under-aroused by sensory input. Most autistic children have some combination of sensory-seeking and sensory-averse behaviors. They might do things like touch other people or fixate on a spinning object because their bodies seek sensory input. When they aim to avoid or minimize sensory input, they might cover their ears in a loud environment, refuse to play with messy materials, or engage in physical activities that involve moving their bodies out of an upright position. Children on the autism spectrum also tend to have difficulty registering the body's internal signals, and they might have trouble recognizing when they have to go to the bathroom or when they feel hungry, thirsty, or tired.

In Matthew's case, sensory issues affect his ability to self-regulate when he misses the opportunity to go outside. Having time to run, climb, and jump is key for satisfying Matthew's need for different kinds of sensory input. Because he is not able to engage in any physical exercise or activities that stimulate his nervous system, Matthew feels out of sorts. This nagging sense of discomfort puts a strain on his emotional resources. As the morning wears on, his capacity to cope with stressful situations rapidly diminishes.

ANXIETY AND STRESS IN AUTISTIC CHILDREN

Think of a time when you felt anxious, perhaps due to an upcoming exam, interview, or event such as meeting your potential in-laws for the first time. Anxiety can permeate everything you do, so that even simple tasks, such as getting dressed, feel difficult or nearly impossible. Children on the autism spectrum frequently have increased anxiety and stress, and these feelings make it hard for them to stay regulated, to find the state where they feel comfortable (Stoddart, 2005).

When a child is faced with a task he finds hard, like throwing a ball or interacting with a peer, his increased anxiety can make such tasks feel even more demanding or frustrating. Because we might not sense the child's underlying anxiety, we might feel surprised if he suddenly gets upset. To us, it looks like the child's strong reaction comes out of nowhere. In reality, however, the child has been struggling to manage his anxiety for some time, and his feelings eventually reach the tipping point. He then becomes overwhelmed and reacts to the situation by screaming, yelling, or crying.

In our earlier example, Matthew—to the teacher's surprise—responds with this same highly reactive behavior when he is directed to the art center. Mrs. Landry does not realize that Matthew's extreme anger and sadness result from his underlying anxiety about art, an activity that is difficult for him.

Although autistic children tend to experience higher levels of generalized anxiety, they also feel anxious because of the specific challenges they often experience. As we have seen, these challenges can stem from sensory issues, delayed motor skills, or difficulty with organizing tasks. It can also be hard for autistic children to recognize and express their feelings, understand other people's perspectives, and manage unexpected changes to their routine. Such challenges increase children's stress and anxiety, affecting their developing self-esteem and self-concept.

Many perceive themselves as different from their peers and ponder questions like, "Why can't I make friends? Why can't I do that when it's so easy for everyone else? What's wrong with me?" Imagine how a child might feel about himself when he struggles to make friends, manage his emotions, and communicate his needs and wants—skills that are essential in successfully navigating the world.

These difficulties can exacerbate elevated levels of anxiety in a child, leading to a sense of alienation and inadequacy—feelings that can erupt in challenging behavior. When such upheaval occurs, it is distressing for everyone involved, but it is most harmful to the child himself.

Thinking back to three-year-old Joseph, who tickles his peers when he approaches them, we see that he becomes increasingly frustrated when his attempts at social interaction repeatedly backfire. Although Joseph thinks he's being friendly, his overtures of kindness, as he sees them, are met with outright rejection. Sometimes, the other kids harshly command him to stop; at other times, they move away when they see Joseph approach. As a result of these unsuccessful exchanges, Joseph begins to feel like it's pointless to try to play with his peers. He perceives himself as an outcast who is unworthy of friends.

This heightened sense of despair decreases his ability to self-regulate. When his parents want to take him to the playground, for instance, Joseph feels so anxious that he refuses to go, and he kicks and screams if his mom or dad tries to scoop him up to head out of the house. Eventually, the family just stops trying to go to the park, and Joseph's parents can't understand why he doesn't want to run around and play outside with the other kids.

During times when Joseph can't avoid his peers, like during recess at school, he often attempts to withdraw socially and keep to himself. Occasionally he reaches out to the other kids but does so in an antagonistic way, calling his classmates names or taking their toys from them. Joseph engages in these negative actions not because he's a mean kid or a bully, but because he's trying to avoid having his feelings hurt again. He projects his emotions of isolation and pain outward, rejecting his peers before they can reject him. From this defensive and anxious perspective, Joseph sometimes loses control, possibly hitting his peers and acting aggressively toward the adults who try to correct him. This behavior earns him extended periods of time-out and further alienates him from his peers.

These episodes of extreme behavior also harm Joseph's self-esteem. On top of the strenuous emotions he experiences, Joseph feels ashamed for losing his cool and lashing out at others. Each time one of these events occurs, a child potentially perceives himself as a bad kid who is out of control.

Because these negative feelings can accumulate, repeated experiences of dysregulation can seriously damage a child's self-worth.

THE TAKEAWAY

We focus on self-regulation as the overarching premise of this book because it is a key concept that encompasses the varied challenges associated with autism. Self-regulation, moreover, is also a foundational skill that takes priority over other areas of need often seen in children with autism. Without the ability to self-regulate, autistic children cannot learn effectively, benefit from disciplinary interventions, or manage the strong emotions and sensory experiences that stem from their neurological differences. The challenges that autistic children face every day are rooted in this distinctive neurology. It is essential for parents and teachers to understand that autistic children have difficulty with processing, verbalizing, and modulating emotions due to differences in brain structure and neural connectivity.

Although we want children to participate in daily activities and complete assigned tasks, we need to recognize that even fun events and projects can pose unique challenges for autistic children. When we see a child becoming dysregulated and struggling to fulfill a demand, our job is not to insist that he complete the task at hand, but to help him reestablish emotional equilibrium. Remembering Ross Greene's mantra that "kids do well if they can," we should take the child's feelings seriously and seek to understand his perspective. This means working with him to find a different approach to the activity, whether that involves helping him with it, postponing it, or setting it aside completely.

If a child does not have the skills that are necessary for completing a task, we should not insist that he comply with the demand, for that insistence will result only in frustration and failure for everyone involved. Rather, we should help the child develop the skills he needs over time, while also remaining focused on the most important skill of all—the capacity to self-regulate.

Self-regulation is the top priority not only for helping an autistic child get through the day, but also for ensuring his well-being in the long term. Without self-regulation—that is, without feeling in control of his emotions and behavior—a child is not able to follow directions, complete tasks, or get along with others. In other words, without self-regulation, it is virtually impossible to function successfully in a social environment. Our goal is to help children self-regulate so that they can learn and interact effectively with others. But how can we help children self-regulate? That is our next topic.

II

SETTING CHILDREN
UP FOR SUCCESS

We can help autistic children manage their emotions and behavior by employing a series of fundamental techniques that will set them up for success in early learning environments and other settings as well. The chapters that follow explore three overarching strategies that are essential to promoting self-regulation: adjusting learning experiences and the environment; emphasizing structure and consistency; and fostering collaboration and emotional awareness. These are foundational strategies that inform our overall approach to helping autistic children be successful. The core concepts discussed in this section remain important throughout the book as we refine key techniques and tailor them both to fit specific situations and to target specific skills.

In offering a general overview of the vital interventions we can make to support self-regulation, we want to stress the importance of being proactive. Before we ask children to enter into a specific situation or activity, we need to have a basic understanding of the strong emotions and challenges they might experience. We also need to establish a plan that seeks to mitigate potential difficulties and that provides support in the areas where children need it. In short, we must set children up for success.

Our advance preparation and sensitivity to a child's needs are a worthwhile investment. It takes only a little extra time and effort to lay the groundwork for a child to feel competent and capable. If a child can have a smooth and positive experience while working on a task or participating in an event, then we have a win–win situation for everyone involved. The child feels a sense of accomplishment, and the people around him share in that success, enjoying the benefits of being with a contented child in a calm environment.

3

ADJUST LEARNING EXPERIENCES AND THE ENVIRONMENT

It's important to begin every day with the mind-set that we need to set children up for success. This goal means that we should meet the child at his comfort level and avoid placing demands on him that we know he can't yet fulfill—demands that likely will trigger a tantrum or meltdown. Does this mean we can never challenge autistic children? No. It simply means that we need to see their growth and emotional development as a process, and that process evolves differently for every child.

Children make progress most readily if we challenge them to learn and grow in an environment where they can maintain self-regulation. The key is to make demands that are congruent with the child's abilities. Create an environment where the child feels competent and comfortable, then demands can be slowly increased.

For example, Tiyana, a four-year-old, struggles to play interactively with her parents and siblings. She prefers to watch YouTube videos on her iPad, and she spends far too much time absorbed in her electronics, not engaging with members of her family. Her parents have set a timer on the iPad, but Tiyana always becomes upset when she's reached her limit and grows increasingly agitated when her parents direct her to play something else. She isn't able to transition smoothly to another type of play activity, and she struggles with taking initiative to find something else to do even when her parents and sisters want to play with her.

To help increase Tiyana's self-regulation in trying different games, her parents help her create an activity book. Her father walks around the house with her, taking pictures of all the different toys and activities that are available. He talks with excitement about all the things they can play with family and friends. He then prints out the pictures, and Tiyana helps to create a "fun book" depicting choices of activities ranging from building Legos and finger painting to playing dress-up and having a tea party. The photos prove particularly useful in this instance because Tiyana does not yet read. Once the book is complete, Tiyana feels proud, and she decorates it with her favorite stickers. In this way, Tiyana takes ownership of the "fun book" and the ideas therein.

On the next occasion when Tiyana reaches the time limit on the iPad, her parents refer her to the "fun book" to help her remain calm and take initiative in choosing another activity. After paging through the book and seeing several possibilities, she ultimately decides that she and her family should build a fort in their den with blankets and pillows.

Having a predetermined list makes it much easier for Tiyana to choose a new activity and leave the iPad behind. She feels more comfortable now not only because the photos serve as a concrete reminder that other activities are fun, but also because she's empowered to make the decision about what to play next. As a result, Tiyana can move on to interactive play with increased self-regulation. Her parents have set Tiyana up for success by giving her a way to initiate new forms of play while feeling calm and in control.

Here's an in-school example that similarly shows how we can set children up for success by making small adjustments to activities and the environment. Four-year-old Ethan has difficulty attending to circle time at the start of the school year. He frequently stays in another area of the classroom while his peers sit attentively singing the morning song and going over the calendar and weather. Although the teacher could insist that Ethan join circle time and perhaps attempt to hold him on her lap, she senses that he is avoiding the activity because he is anxious about something. She recognizes that for Ethan, circle time presents a demand that feels overly challenging to him. She also knows that if she insists that he join the activity, Ethan's anxiety will only increase. This outcome won't help Ethan join the group; in fact, it will likely make him even *more* resistant to circle time.

Ethan's teacher decides to take a different approach by setting him up for success. She wants Ethan to join the group and to be engaged with the class activities, but she does not attempt to force him into circle time. However, she also does not allow him to wander throughout the classroom doing whatever he wants. Instead, she creates an environment where Ethan can join circle time when he feels capable of meeting that demand. The teacher tells Ethan that she would love to have him join the group and that she will wait for him to become part of circle time when he feels ready. She creates a "listening spot" near the circle time area, providing a space for Ethan where he can be safe and comfortable while still hearing what is happening. She places hand fidgets and a few other items in the area to offer Ethan sensory stimulation and to make the "listening spot" appealing to him.

Sitting in this spot, Ethan listens when his class is having circle time, and, before long, his teacher finds that he begins to talk, later in the day, about the topics that his classmates discussed. After several weeks, Ethan begins to join circle time about halfway through the activity. Eventually, he joins circle time from the beginning. Once he is given time to adjust to school and to observe activities from a safe distance, he feels comfortable in becoming part of the class activity.

By giving Ethan time and space, the teacher initially encourages him to maintain self-regulation during an anxiety-provoking situation. At the same time, she also creates an environment where she can challenge Ethan, gently leading him to overcome his anxiety and participate in circle time along with the rest of the class.

As this example suggests, in setting a child up for success, we not only create opportunities for the child to learn and grow, but we maximize the chances that the child will seize those opportunities and be successful in overcoming a particular challenge. The key is to encourage the child to meet a difficult demand while also making it possible for him to manage the potentially overwhelming emotions he feels.

It's important to recognize that children do not usually refuse to participate in activities simply out of willfulness or noncompliance. A child's refusal is most likely an attempt to maintain self-regulation in the face of a situation that feels scary, overwhelming, or impossible to him. For this reason, it's critical to recognize the child's need to feel safe and in control. We can help the child stretch to do new things while also acknowledging that he can't effectively participate in an activity where he does not feel secure. Below, we offer some easy ways to set children up for success by adjusting learning experiences and the environment.

> **In general, autistic children don't refuse to join activities out of willfulness or noncompliance.**

USE PICTURES

Autistic children are frequently visual thinkers (Grandin, 1995). It's therefore helpful to use visual cues to accompany verbal instructions. Visual cues allow individuals to process information with different parts of the brain. Rather than expecting children to learn and perceive things through auditory input alone, we can use pictures to offer instruction in another format geared toward students whose brains are more efficient at processing visual material. In this way, pictures can help to make up for auditory processing challenges, leading to greater clarity and understanding—outcomes that, in turn, support the goal of self-regulation.

Although pictures can be incorporated into virtually any strategy aimed at supporting self-regulation, we offer specific ways to use pictures to facilitate learning and to help all children be successful. Use pictures to

1. *Depict rules.* Use one picture for each major rule at home or in the classroom. For example, a picture might feature a child sitting at the kitchen table to eat or raising his hand to ask a question.
2. *Create a visual schedule.* Use a different picture to denote each activity. For example, at home, create a visual schedule for the morning routine that shows the different steps of getting dressed, eating breakfast, and brushing teeth. At school, create a visual schedule laying out the different activities such as circle time, outdoor play, snack time, and centers.
3. *Delineate boundaries.* If three children are allowed in a particular "center" or activity area at school, use a picture to display three children in this area. Or at home, for example, create an art corner and put pictures on bins to designate where crayons, markers, and other art supplies belong. In any location, you can also use a "do not enter" sign with a graphic to signify areas that are off-limits.
4. *Preview upcoming events.* For example, when telling children about a fire drill scheduled for later in the day at school, show pictures of children lining up and gathering at the designated the location. Likewise, at home, when planning a visit to a relative's house, use pictures to show children where you are going and what the expectations are there.
5. *Encourage children to make a choice.* For example, ask a child to choose a song for circle time. Each song is depicted by a picture and is attached with Velcro to a "choice board." Similarly, during playtime at home, ask the child to choose a game from a selection of pictures or from her activity book as previously described.
6. *Help children transition easily from one space to another.* In a busy classroom, it can be helpful to have a child carry a picture of the play area she is headed to and deposit it in a basket stationed at the new play space. Also use pictures to anticipate any transitions that prove to be challenging at home. For example, at bath time, give the child a picture of a rubber duck that she can take to the bathroom as a cue to find her own rubber duck to play with in the tub.

7. *Explain different coping skills.* Show children different ways that they can deal with anger, frustration, and other strong emotions. For example, have them use a break card, which is a small card with a picture of a place in that setting where the child can take a break and regain self-regulation. This card reminds children that taking a break is a useful coping skill. Break cards will be described in further detail in chapter 4.

FACILITATE PLANNING AND ORGANIZATION

Planning and organization can be challenging for many children on the autism spectrum who have decreased executive functioning skills. These children might have difficulty with multistep activities that require logical thinking, decision making, and foreseeing the different stages of a task. Fine motor and gross motor development can also be delayed in autistic children, making it hard for them to understand how their bodies are positioned in space (Shannon, 2011). They might also struggle to maintain balance and to move in a controlled and coordinated way. Writing, drawing, and cutting—activities that many kids enjoy—are often exercises in frustration and disappointment for children on the autism spectrum.

We can readily ease some of these challenges by adjusting the physical environment at home or in the classroom. For example, getting ready for bed might seem like a straightforward task, but autistic children, like many neurotypical children, may struggle when it comes to settling down for the night. Though bedtime can present a range of challenges, there are a number of ways that parents can help children prepare for sleep simply by making adjustments to the environment.

Most simply, parents can make sure that the child's bedroom is relatively organized by putting away toys and other objects that are likely to be a source of distraction. We want the atmosphere of the room to signal that it's time to quiet down, and the environment should facilitate the ultimate goal of getting to sleep. After putting toys away, it's also helpful to lay out the items needed for the bedtime routine. Present two pairs of pajamas and let the child choose one. Leave out three short books so that he can pick two to read before going to sleep. Parents can also adjust the environment at bedtime by turning down the lights, playing soft music, or spraying a calming scent if the child finds that appealing.

In the school environment, it's important for teachers to define the boundaries in the classroom and to designate discrete play areas so that children have a clear understanding of where they are allowed to go, how many children are allowed in an area, and what they are allowed to touch. The strategy of using pictures, as discussed above, can be helpful in making these designations clear. For example, classrooms can use visual clues to indicate where children should sit on the floor, and teachers can place pictures on bins to indicate what is in each container.

Children should be able to move easily from one place to another in the classroom. The pathways between centers should be clear to facilitate movement. As discussed earlier, we also can offer support in activities like circle time, when we often see autistic children lying down or rolling around on the floor only minutes after being instructed to sit. Although such actions can be misconstrued as inattentive or disrespectful behavior, the reality is that many autistic children lack core muscle strength, making it difficult and sometimes even painful for them to hold up their bodies for any significant amount of time.

To remedy this problem, we can let a child use a small beanbag or Howda chair (www.howda.com). The child then has a designated place to sit, and his body will be more stable since the chair supports his back and core muscles. For art activities and other seated tasks, we can organize the work environment to minimize potential distractions or points of confusion. When preparing crafts, for example, restrict the number of objects that are presented to the child and arrange the necessary supplies in way that reduces clutter. Having too many items piled up on a table can crowd a child's vision and increase his disorganization.

In addition to adjusting work materials and physical space, we can also offer other kinds of support when we ask children to engage in art projects, writing, and other fine motor tasks that might seem unappealing. We can easily make a number of accommodations so that a task such as making Valentine's Day cards seems manageable.

1. *Review coping skills before beginning the activity and make sure the child knows that he can take a break.* For example, start by saying, "Your grandpa is going to love this card! Sometimes making a card can be a little tricky. If you feel frustrated, say 'I want a break.'"
2. *Give directions in short, concise phrases.* For example, tell the child, "Pick what color you want—red or pink."
3. *Use "chunking" to break tasks into smaller, more manageable steps.* For example, simply telling a child to trace a heart can be confusing because it's an action that requires coordination, organization, and the execution of multiple steps. It's effective to divide the task into discrete parts, telling the child: "First, put the piece of construction

paper on the table. Second, place the cardboard heart in the middle. Now, take the pencil and draw around the heart."

4. *Offer options and choices.* For example, ask the child, "Do you want to use lace on your valentine or glitter?" Choices help children feel more in control.

5. *Provide one-on-one help while sitting next to the child on his level.* You might say, "It's cool doing this project with you. I see that it's tricky to cut the top, curvy lines on the heart. How about we work on that part together?"

6. *Offer encouragement and praise for each small accomplishment.* You could say, "I love the sticker you chose, and it looks great right where you put it."

7. *Reward trying.* Tell the child, for example, "You are working so hard on this card! Grandpa is going to be so impressed by everything you're doing to make it for him." This encouragement also reminds the child of the outcome of the task.

8. *Offer reminders to ask for help.* You can say, "Your valentine is looking great! I'm right here to help you if need it."

It's perhaps most important to set up the task so that the child feels capable of doing it. If it looks impossible, chances are very low that he will try it, so offer assistance that makes the task seem doable. Give assurances by telling the child, "I'll be right here" or "If anything is tricky, let me know." Hand-over-hand assistance can be helpful at times. In other instances, the adult can complete the parts of the task that are overly challenging and leave the parts of the task that the child can complete independently. As the child masters more skills, the adult can do fewer parts of the task.

In the end, the goal is to maintain self-regulation, not to complete a designated task or activity. We want the child to participate and feel a sense of accomplishment even if he does not produce a fully finished project. A piece of artwork born out of deep frustration and feelings of incompetence does not offer children much incentive to undertake similar activities in the future. By decreasing anxiety and facilitating a successful experience, we can help the child gain confidence and learn to enjoy activities they find challenging.

OFFER INCENTIVES AND REWARDS

As we have seen, children on the autism spectrum tend to have difficulty completing nonpreferred tasks due to increased anxiety and delayed skills in various areas. Because tasks can be so much more confusing and demanding for children with autism, they may need extra incentives to participate in certain activities. Children on the autism spectrum frequently want to know "What's in it for me?" It may not be enough motivation for autistic children to engage in a task simply because they have been instructed to do so. Their perspective can be more focused on their own wants and needs, which are magnified by heightened anxiety and sensitivity to their environment.

They may view some tasks as extremely challenging, annoying, or even tortuous, and they want to understand why they should bother in the first place. In these cases, it can be effective to use incentives to encourage children to engage in a difficult or nonpreferred activity without spiraling into extreme dysregulation. For example, a parent or teacher might use the "if–then" technique and tell a child: "*If* you finish this drawing, *then* we will go outside." It's helpful to pair nonpreferred activities with preferred activities. Set up a daily schedule so that more difficult, challenging tasks are followed by activities that the child finds enjoyable.

Offering positive reinforcement for positive behavior is also effective for autistic children as it is for neurotypical children. If you want a positive behavior to increase, reward it. Even small tokens, especially if given frequently, can show that good things happen when children act in positive ways. They see concretely that there is something in it for them by engaging in requested and desirable behavior. Rewards can therefore increase their motivation and help them participate successfully in the day's activities—accomplishments that also promote self-regulation.

Pair nonpreferred activities with preferred activities as an incentive for participating in tasks that are challenging or anxiety inducing.

Positive reinforcement for children with autism needs to be tangible; that is, something they can see, touch, feel, or eat. Here are some options.

1. *Star chart.* The child receives stars for targeted, positive behavior such as following directions. The stars can be redeemed for specified rewards that are meaningful for the child. After earning three stars, the child can have a fruit gummy, one of his favorite foods.
2. *Point chart.* The child earns points for targeted, positive behavior, and the points can be redeemed for specified rewards that are meaningful for the child. For example, at either home or school, the child gets a point for speaking politely and using respectful language. Five points can be traded for five minutes of iPad time at school or TV time at home (or two of the child's favorite activities).
3. *Reward choice board.* The child chooses what reward he would like to earn for completing a certain task or engaging in a targeted,

positive behavior. He then earns it immediately upon completion of the goal. Rewards are displayed in picture form on a small clipboard and doled out as frequently as needed. Enlist the child's help in developing the possible rewards to make sure that they're tailored to his individual preferences. For example, a three-year-old might find that stickers are a great reward, whereas a six-year-old might like a small toy or book.

4. *Instant edible reward.* The child is rewarded with an edible treat that can be eaten quickly, such as a pretzel or small piece of candy, like an M&M or Skittle, upon completion of the desired behavior/task. Instant edible rewards should be awarded with whatever frequency is needed to maintain the desired behavior.

5. *Combined schedule and reward board.* Each activity on the child's schedule correlates with a specific reward also depicted on the board. The child receives the reward when the activity/targeted behavior is completed. For example, at school, a child can earn a ticket for sitting with the class at circle time or for working on the daily art project. The tickets can be traded for prizes kept in a small chest in the classroom. At home, a child can put a marble in a clear cup each time he does something like washing his hands before dinner or sitting at the table for a designated period of time. Parents can assign a value to each marble so that one equals 10 cents or five minutes of extra story time and so forth.

In sum, by making simple adjustments to a child's learning experience and environment, we can go a long way toward setting him up for success. We can help autistic children feel more secure at home and at school by capitalizing on their visual processing skills and using pictures whenever possible to convey expectations, to ease transitions, and to offer coping strategies.

To support autistic children with planning and organization, we can make simple changes not only to the physical environment and work space, but also to the nature of the work itself. For example, we can break activities up into small steps, we can offer direct assistance and support when needed, and we can often let children choose how to complete or engage in a task. Finally, teachers and parents can affirm the value of a child's positive behavior and engagement by offering him rewards that concretely recognize and reinforce his hard work and accomplishments. These proactive techniques are basic yet crucial accommodations that we can implement to help autistic children thrive at school and at home. Keeping this same goal in mind, the next chapter turns to the topics of structure and consistency, which are also key elements for setting children up for success.

4

EMPHASIZE STRUCTURE AND CONSISTENCY

The Autistic Child Needs to Know "What Are We Doing?"

Imagine that you've lost your planner and you can't remember everything you're supposed to do in the course of the day. You know that you have several appointments and events scheduled—that you have certain obligations—but you can't remember the details and you don't know how you'll ever be able to recover the missing information you need. How would you react? Chances are you would feel upset, anxious, frustrated, or annoyed.

Though it's easy enough to go out and buy a new planner, replacing the lost object does not help at all because the missing planner represents a larger loss—the loss of predictability. People like to know what is going to happen. They feel grounded and secure when they have a sense of what events and activities are on the horizon. This desire for certainty extends into many aspects of human life. For example, it explains why chain restaurants all look the same, and why they feature standardized menus across the country. People find this sense of uniformity and familiarity appealing. They take comfort in knowing what to expect.

Children on the autism spectrum have a particularly strong need to know what to expect. Having an idea of what is going to happen each day gives them a sense of control over their environment. Daily rituals and patterns help them feel secure. As Bill Stillman, a writer with autism explains, "There is safety in sameness and comfort in what is familiar" (Stillman, 2002, 80). Because uncertainty raises anxiety, having a routine for the day helps children with autism self-regulate. They thrive in a daily structure where the expectations are clear and predictable.

Of course, there are times when things do not go as planned, and we find ourselves scrambling to deal with eventualities we have not anticipated. Just as the lack of routine feels highly destabilizing for most people, the

31

unexpected disruption of a routine can be equally distressing. For example, now imagine that you walk out of your house to drive to work and find that your car is missing. After ruling out other possibilities, you realize that your car has been stolen. You begin to feel panicked. You have an important meeting that you can't miss. You also need a car for a family vacation that starts in two days. What are you going to do? How are you going to deal with the problem of the stolen car while also fulfilling all your other responsibilities? Realizing that the stolen car disrupts many aspects of your life, you feel overwhelmed and upset. As this example suggests, unwanted surprises can be troubling, creating extra demands at the same time we are expected to meet the obligations already in place.

This experience offers a glimpse into how children on the autism spectrum feel when their routines are thrown off even in minor ways. Children with autism acutely feel the effects of disruption and unpredictability. Because it's impossible to avoid unexpected situations, it's essential to help autistic children develop tools for coping with the inevitability of change. At the same time, though, we can also strive to be consistent in the aspects of life that we can control. There are many ways to develop a clear routine and promote structure, and several specific techniques follow.

CREATE A VISUAL SCHEDULE

Post a schedule for the day using pictures to represent different activities. Review the schedule at the beginning of each day, as this activity promotes a sense of control and security. Note, however, that sometimes children on the autism spectrum may feel overwhelmed by a list of all the day's potentially daunting activities. In this case it's best to develop an individualized schedule that might include more frequent breaks. Encourage participation in activities in which the child can be successful, and do not force activities that are overly demanding. As the child gains more skills, these tasks can be added.

Give the child a copy of her own visual schedule (perhaps on a small clipboard) with a box next to each item so that she can check off the box when she has completed an activity. This process increases the child's sense of control and allows her to see what she has finished, what is coming next, and how many activities are still left to complete. Rewards can be listed on the chart for completing each activity, and, in this way, the visual schedule can also increase a child's sense of accomplishment (see the appendix for visual schedule resources).

PREVIEWING IS PARAMOUNT

To promote self-regulation, we can preview an activity by going over information, rules, and expectations prior to the start of the event. Previewing helps reduce a child's anxiety because he learns what to expect and gains a sense of predictability about something that is otherwise unknown. Previewing also gives the child time to ask questions and process upcoming events before he becomes involved in them.

When we give a child advance information about an event, we also increase the likelihood that he will cooperate and be a good listener because he learns what the rules are and how to behave accordingly. In essence, previewing promotes self-regulation because it enables people to feel calm and more in control of an upcoming situation (Nason, 2014). It's important to preview activities, rules, and expectations, especially when we can anticipate changes to the routine and events that are out of the ordinary.

Even if there are no special occasions on the horizon, previewing can also be a useful tool for reminding children of daily rules and expectations. For example, in their classrooms, teachers can clearly display rules in picture form and ask the children to name a rule by pointing to a specific picture. It's possible to go a step further and to use previewing to explain why we need certain rules in the first place. For example, use a picture of a child walking in the classroom to explain the rule, "Walk, don't run." Ask the children what the picture means in order to draw out the underlying reason for the rule—that people might get hurt if we run in the classroom because we could bump into each other or trip over something.

Children are naturally inquisitive and want to understand why things happen. We can increase their understanding of the world and promote self-regulation by explaining why certain rules and directions are in place. Previewing is also valuable for explaining specific tasks. Before starting an activity, go over the expectations with the child. For children with autism, it may not be obvious that the rules for an art project are inherently different from the rules for something like outdoor play. In general, previewing helps children know what is expected, and when they have a sense of what is to come, they feel calmer, more in control, and ready to participate in the activity at hand.

ANTICIPATE TRANSITIONS

Imagine, after arriving at work, that your boss suddenly tells you that you must work in a different place for the day due to construction. You begin thinking about all the items you need to move from your desk to an unfamiliar part of the building. Your files, computer equipment, and office supplies are arranged in the way you like them, but everything will be disorganized once you move it to a new location. You realize how much this change will disrupt your day, especially since you were planning to finish a big project that you've been working on for weeks. This transition, you decide, is totally annoying and inconvenient. It disrupts the work you need to do, interfering with your plans to complete an assignment that your boss is expecting.

Even relatively minor transitions can provoke such feelings in autistic children who need more time to process change (Nason, 2014). Think about the many transitions a child must make during a single day at school. First, he has to enter the busy classroom in the morning and move to a designated area or center. As the day progresses, sometimes he must stay put until he finishes and cleans up his work. At other times, however, he needs to leave a project incomplete to move on to the next scheduled activity. When leaving the classroom, he has to line up calmly, perhaps waiting for the whole class to be quiet before they can head outside. During afternoon dismissal, he must pack up and switch gears to make the transition from school to home.

On any given day, a child also has to be prepared to handle special programs and trips as well as the possibility of new students or adults entering the environment. Children on the autism spectrum need extra time to deal with all these transitions. Change is difficult for them because, as we have seen, they like sameness and find comfort and security in a routine. Offering extra time and anticipating changes are key techniques for helping autistic children make transitions smoothly. Let's look at some examples that demonstrate this strategy.

A few months ago, four-year-old Paige became extremely upset before leaving the house for a doctor's appointment. She was happily watching her favorite movie when her mother announced that it was time for them to head to the doctor's office. At first, Paige ignored her mother, but after being reminded to turn off the TV a few times, Paige eventually shouted that she wasn't going anywhere until her movie ended. Paige's mother initially tried reasoning with her, noting that she didn't have to watch the whole movie because she already had seen it many times. But this response only made Paige more resistant to leaving. Her mother ended up having to wrestle the remote out of Paige's hand, turn off the TV herself, and carry Paige, kicking and screaming, to the car.

The next time Paige has a doctor's appointment, her mother approaches the situation differently. First thing in the morning, she reviews the schedule for the day, letting Paige know that after she watches TV for a little while, she has to see the doctor. Then, after the appointment, they'll come home for lunch. Next, she helps Paige pick a short movie to watch so that she can finish the film before they need to leave and still have enough time to make the transition without rushing. In most cases, pushing an autistic child to move quickly only makes transitions more difficult.

Once Paige's movie ends, her mother brings her coat to her, praising Paige for putting it on and getting ready to go like a "big girl." Her mother also gives Paige a favorite toy to hold, suggesting that she show it to the doctor once they arrive for the appointment. Additionally, Paige's mother tells her that if she's a good cooperator at the doctor's office, as a special treat, she can eat lunch in front of the TV when they return home. By "sandwiching" the doctor's appointment between events that Paige enjoys, her mother eases the transition and makes the nonpreferred activity feel more tolerable.

Let's look at another example, this time exploring how to help a child cope with multiple transitions at school. Upon arriving in the morning, Billy has difficulty entering the classroom and following the teacher's directive to sit down at the table with the other teacher to begin painting parts of a project they will assemble later in the day. He wants to play cars on the carpet, and he isn't a fan of painting. However, when he's offered time to adjust to the classroom environment, spending five to ten minutes playing on his own, he then feels ready to do some painting.

Once he gets involved in the project, he becomes so invested in making his painting perfect that he needs extra time to wrap up his work. When the activity has to come to an end, the teacher gives him five-minute, three-minute, and one-minute warnings about the impending transition, helping him process that his time for painting is just about over. The teacher also quietly reminds Billy about the next activity, making sure to emphasize something that he will look forward to doing. The teacher's prompts and reminders enable Billy to move on to the next activity while also remaining calm, an outcome that wouldn't have been possible if the teacher had suddenly announced that painting time was over.

Other ways of increasing predictability and reducing the anxiety associated with transitions might include making use of a visual timer. By setting up a timer and displaying it clearly, parents, teachers, or other adults can enable children to see how much time is left for the designated activity. Timers also help reduce potential power struggles between children and adults because they are an object—a neutral third party, so to speak—not a person with whom one can argue.

BUILD IN BREAKS

Another important time-related strategy to help children stay regulated is to make sure that breaks are part of the daily structure. In some cases, breaks can be planned as preemptive opportunities for downtime when we know that a child's energy level is likely to wane. Breaks also might happen spontaneously to offer a child time apart when she begins to show signs of frustration or agitation. Whether they are preplanned or happen in the moment, breaks need to be a recognizable and acceptable part of daily life.

Autistic children generally need more time to process their thoughts and feelings, and we want to encourage them to take the space they need rather than allowing their emotions to boil over. When children with autism feel frustrated or need extra processing time, they frequently prefer to do that on their own without having to face additional demands or feel scrutinized by others. For example, four-year-old Jack always seeks time alone when he is upset, but the adults who are present keep talking to Jack and trying to help him when he shows signs of distress. Their response makes Jack angry, and at one point, he yells at the grown-ups, telling them to be quiet and leave him alone. When they finally back off, the adults see that Jack calms down rather quickly, and it becomes clear that he knows what he needs—time and space to self-regulate without anyone interacting with him.

Children on the autism spectrum should have a designated break area, or "break spot" as it's sometimes labeled. At home, this can be a space in the child's bedroom, or another quiet place where the child can relax and be away from others. In a classroom, this should be a small area on the periphery that is separate from the other children and activity centers but still within view of an adult. A corner or small nook of a room is ideal. The break spot should have a beanbag chair or other comfortable place to sit, along with some preferred activities such as puzzles and books. Items that promote sensory stimulation can also be useful, including hand fidgets and other toys that the child can squeeze.

Introduce the break spot when the child is calm and explain that it is a resource to help him. It's not time-out; it's not a punishment. Let the child know that it's available to him whenever he needs it. Encourage the child to suggest which calming items he would like to put in his break spot.

It's often difficult for children with autism to recognize when they need downtime. Sometimes when a child becomes upset, it proves difficult to verbalize the thought, "I need a break." In this case, verbal or visual prompts may encourage children to use the break spot. A "break card" featuring a picture of the break spot can be used to show the child that it's time to go to her quiet space. The child can keep the break card in her possession, and she can use it to indicate to a parent or teacher that she needs some time to herself. When the child has her own break card, she feels more in control and she has a concrete way of dealing with frustration, anger, and anxiety. The card empowers her to use her break spot and to make good choices that increase self-regulation. For example, six-year-old Maria becomes angry after her little brother rips her drawing. She is about to hit him when her father hands her the break card. She takes it, looks at it, and then looks at her father, who says, "That might be a good choice right about now. I'll help you talk to your brother when you're ready to use words." Maria then stomps away to her bedroom, her designated break spot.

Some people may worry that a child will use the break spot as a means of avoiding work she needs to complete or escaping activities that she doesn't like. In our experience, children usually have good reasons for resisting an activity, so we should first try to determine the root cause of a child's resistance. When we address the underlying problem, then we can redirect the child to the task once she's calm and has the necessary support.

Overall, we must remember that learning to self-regulate is not an escape from hard work—it *is* hard work, work that is vital in helping autistic children feel productive and successful in life. It's always more important to help children reach the long-term goal of being able to manage their feelings than to insist that they complete a task in a given moment. Being able to recognize their need for a break is a key skill that we want autistic children to develop.

All of the strategies in this chapter are aimed at helping children feel secure and knowledgeable as they move through the different activities and events of daily life. Emphasizing structure and consistency is key in this regard. In addition to providing children with a visual schedule, we can preview events with them and anticipate transitions so that they won't feel surprised or upset when it's time to end an activity they may be engrossed in.

> It's always more important to help children reach the long-term goal of being able to manage their feelings than to insist that they complete a task in a given moment.

At any given moment, we want children to know the answers to the questions "what are we doing?" and "what's going to happen next?" We can greatly decrease their anxiety by doing our best to make sure that they know what to expect. Part of what we want children to expect is the opportunity to take a break when they need extra time to process information or retreat from a highly stimulating environment.

Knowing when to seek downtime is an important skill, one that ultimately supports structure and routine by enabling a child to get through the day without shutting down altogether or devolving into significant stretches of challenging behavior. In emphasizing routine and structure, we set autistic children up for success by helping them to feel competent and secure in everyday life. The next chapter, which focuses on collaboration and emotional awareness, offers another set of key strategies that also builds a child's sense of security and lays a foundation for successful interaction in the world.

5

FOSTER COLLABORATION
AND EMOTIONAL AWARENESS

As we have described, children on the autism spectrum can be easily overwhelmed. They tend to become upset and frustrated more readily than their neurotypical peers. The reason for this difficulty can be found in the weak connections between the emotional part of the brain (the amygdala) and the thinking part of the brain (the prefrontal cortex). Because of this neurological difference, it can be hard for autistic children to identify, assess, and modulate their feelings. It's therefore important to teach these children coping skills. We want them to learn how to evaluate their emotional state and take appropriate actions based on their feelings. In this chapter, we show that children can come to recognize and communicate their needs effectively if parents and teachers foster a collaborative relationship with them and work to increase their emotional awareness.

When we interact with autistic children, it's first crucial to acknowledge that they have their own agency and need to feel a sense of control. Let's pause for a minute to reflect on the importance of this point. Ask yourself, as a parent or a teacher, the following question: "What am I in control of?" With some reflection, we see that the answer must be as follows: "I am in control of myself, and to some extent, I am also in control of my environment—my home or my classroom. I can rearrange the furniture, put pictures on the wall, and raise or lower the temperature. Am I in control of other people? No. I can alter my behavior and the environment to influence others, but I am not in control of others."

This lesson is important for everyone to remember in daily life, but especially when working with children on the autism spectrum. We don't want to try to control these children; we want them to control *themselves*. And we can help them do that by altering what we do and by shaping the environment.

A key part of this process is to consistently give children the opportunity to think about their emotions and articulate their needs. We want to encourage feelings of competence in autistic children and affirm their perspectives. In this regard, it is extremely important to involve children in decisions that affect them: "In order to feel safe and comfortable, the child must have control" (Stillman, 2010, 19).

Though many parents and teachers assume that children must follow all directives given by adults, we should remember that our ultimate goal is not to promote a child's unquestioning adherence to any figure of authority. Does this mean that it's not important for children to listen to adults and follow rules? No. It means that with our approach to children, we seek to instill lifelong skills such as self-awareness and the capacity for compromise—skills that people need in order to interact successfully with others in the world. It makes sense, then, as part of the very exercise of adult authority, that we build in opportunities for children to have a sense of control. Children learn the most important social and emotional lessons when they have the chance to articulate their own interests, assume responsibility, and make choices.

> "In order to feel safe and comfortable, the child must have control."—Bill Stillman

In addition to making sure that children have a clear stake in decisions that affect them, we can also offer instruction about feelings and coping skills. Although many children intuitively learn how to recognize and process their emotions, autistic children often face challenges in this arena. They can benefit from explicit lessons that not only explain the nuances of different emotions, but that teach specific coping skills that they can use anywhere.

Below, we describe strategies that help children manage their emotions in situations that might provoke significant dysregulation. These strategies also enable children to develop the skills needed for practicing self-regulation in the long term. With the techniques we describe, we set children up for success by enabling them to begin the emotional work that is necessary for navigating the world—recognizing feelings, articulating their needs, and solving problems in collaboration with others.

OFFER CHOICES

Many times, adults make choices for children out of habit, but we don't have to. Children can develop a sense of competence and act in their own interests when they have the opportunity to take initiative and make choices. In daily activities, there are many ways to offer children choices without causing disruption or undermining adult authority. They can:

- Choose a household or classroom job.
- Choose the song on the radio or a specific activity for circle time.
- Choose to take a break.
- Choose which task to complete first whenever possible.
- Choose a color or object whenever possible.
- Choose a partner when appropriate.
- Choose alternate activities offered by an adult when upset.
- Choose to try something again or to pursue another option when a child makes a mistake on a project. For example, he can use extra scrap paper to practice a drawing, or he can use a pencil instead of a marker.

Children on the autism spectrum need choices and options to maintain self-regulation. If they feel backed into a corner—that is, if they feel that they are stuck without options or without a way out—they are likely to get frustrated, angry, and have a temper tantrum. Offering choices can enable them to perform necessary tasks while also appealing to their need to feel comfortable and in control. When children have options, they also have an opportunity to recognize their needs and find a practicable way to have those needs met.

> **Offering choices promotes self-regulation.**

SOLVE PROBLEMS TOGETHER

Raymond is a four-year-old boy who refuses to put on his swimsuit to go outside for water play on a hot day near the end of the school year. His teacher feels frustrated; she needs to make sure that all the children are ready to go outside, and she is growing more impatient with Raymond's lack of cooperation. After several stern reminders that he needs to get his suit on, the teacher finally warns Raymond that he will lose his favorite afternoon activity, time at the computer, if he does not immediately get dressed for water play. However, this warning only makes Raymond go from feeling agitated to being angry, and he teeters on the edge of having a meltdown. He continues to remain steadfast in refusing to put on his swimsuit at the same time that he now imagines an afternoon without his favorite activity.

As in this scenario, adults sometimes seek to solve a problem with great efficiency by asserting their authority and imposing a consequence for disruptive behavior. At other times, they might rush to solve a problem by offering help or by immediately trying to soothe upset feelings. In many cases, however, these efforts are ineffective because they don't actually *solve* the problem at hand. In fact, we often forget to stop and ask "What's the problem?" If we misinterpret or overlook the problem, we can make the situation worse, not better. It's therefore important to determine what the problem is before trying to solve it. This is particularly true with autistic children who can have different triggers leading to behavior that is easily misconstrued as noncompliant or disrespectful.

A collaborative problem-solving method, such as the one developed by child psychologist Ross Greene, can be useful with children on the autism spectrum. The first step in Greene's plan is empathy, in which the adult first asks the child, "What's up?" to determine the problem. Returning to the example above, the teacher could get down on Raymond's level and say, "I see that you don't want to put your swimsuit on. What's up?" Raymond would then have the opportunity to tell the teacher what's bothering him: "I don't want to put my swimsuit on because I know the water will be cold, and I hate being cold. I'd rather keep my clothes on and stay warm."

Once the child has described the issue, repeat the problem back to him—using his own language—so that he is sure you understand his specific concern. Then the adult can move to step two and "define the problem" by explaining her concern and showing her perspective on the problem. The teacher might say, "I see that you don't want to put your swimsuit on because you don't want to be cold. My worry is that you might get wet accidentally or that you might change your mind about playing in the water once you get outside, and I don't want you to be stuck in wet clothes."

Then the adult can engage in the "invitation step," asking "I wonder what we can do about this problem?" The goal here is to work together to find a solution that satisfies both the child's and the adult's concern. This step gives the child some control, and it encourages him to flex his problem-solving skills. Often the child knows just what might help (Greene, 2014a, 92).

In our example with Raymond, he feels inspired to work with his teacher when he sees that she has a valid concern about his comfort. He suggests that he could put his bathing suit on but still plan to stay away from the water. His teacher agrees that this is a good plan and adds that he can keep his towel with him in case he feels cold and needs to use it like a blanket. In this exchange, the teacher has helped Raymond verbalize the problem and come up with a way to resolve it.

This method also works well at home so that parents and children can resolve conflicts while also maintaining and encouraging emotional regulation. For example, by asking "what's up," a parent can discover that a child who refuses to get dressed in the morning isn't just being difficult or disobedient, but that she feels too cold to get out of her pajamas or that the clothes she has to put on are too scratchy. Or maybe the parent learns that the child is resistant because she is anxious about leaving the house due to a scary billboard she sees every day when they drive out of their neighborhood.

Once parents learn the reasons for their child's behavior and validate their child's feelings, they can go on to express their concerns about that behavior, elaborating on the practical problems that will ensue if, for instance, the child doesn't ultimately get dressed. The next step, as we have seen, is to get the child's perspective in finding a workable solution. Depending on the situation, maybe the parents and child agree to set up a portable heater so that it doesn't feel so cold while getting dressed. Maybe they compromise on different clothes for the child to wear. Or maybe they temporarily find another route out of their neighborhood while also working on the long-term goal of helping the child manage her anxiety.

The important takeaway in any of these cases is that the parents and children can avoid becoming locked in a power struggle that only leads to more conflict and emotional upheaval. Instead, they can solve problems together through reason, empathy, and cooperation—qualities we want to instill in our children.

TEACH ABOUT FEELINGS

All children, not just autistic children, benefit from learning about their feelings by discovering how to identify their emotions and how to cope with strong sensations such as sadness, frustration, or rage. Many of us know adults with anger management problems—people who get angry quickly and who express their feelings by yelling, by screaming, or, in extreme cases, by destroying objects or lashing out physically at other people. It's a challenge, then, not just for children, but for many adults to control their feelings and self-regulate. Learning about feelings from a young age can have a positive impact on a person's entire life, especially children with autism. Though there is a lot of information to cover when teaching children about emotions, we can communicate this material to them effectively by dividing it into four manageable steps.

Step 1: Define Different Emotions

It's important to start with basic principles. Teach what feelings are by defining different emotions. Discuss what distinctive emotional states feel like by connecting feelings to bodily sensations. Also, link feelings to specific events. Highlighting these connections helps children see the relationship between experiences in their life and their own feelings and behavior. For example, a parent or teacher might tell a story about a boy who feels angry because he can't go outside now that it's raining. The adult can explain that "He really wanted to go outside to play. Now that he can't do that, he feels like there is a hot, red rock in his belly. His fists ball up really tightly. He starts yelling that it's not fair that he can't go outside. All of this means that he is mad."

Many autistic children have trouble registering the nuances of emotion. Emotions such as jealousy, impatience, and disappointment easily lose their distinctiveness and may be perceived and expressed as anger or sadness. Children with autism therefore need help with distinguishing one emotion from another. It's easy to incorporate this kind of lesson into an activity like reading at home or during story time in the classroom. While reading a book, pause for a moment to ask how a character is feeling, what that feeling entails, and what caused the character to feel that way.

Autistic children also may be unaware that someone can feel more than one emotion at the same time. Help children recognize this possibility by modeling what it's like to experience multiple feelings. For example, an adult might say, "I felt confused and sad when my dog died. I was confused because I wondered why he died since he didn't seem sick. I was sad because I missed him and wouldn't be able to play with him anymore."

Step 2: Help Children Identify Their Own Feelings

Encourage children to say how they are feeling, making sure they explicitly use a feeling word rather than a nonfeeling word. For example, they should describe themselves as feeling happy, sad, mad, scared, or so forth. They should avoid using more ambiguous terms such as "good," "bad," or "okay."

Teachers and parents can have children identify their emotions on a feelings chart that shows distinct facial expressions for different feelings (see the appendix for resources on feelings charts). This visual guide helps children connect feelings to facial expressions, an act that can be challenging for autistic people who often focus on the individual components of a face rather than the entirety of a facial expression (Attwood, 2007).

When teaching about emotions, it's crucial to validate all feelings. This message is clear and simple: *your feelings are your own and it's okay to feel however you feel.* A simple way to validate feelings is to reflect back to the child what you heard him say. If he says that he is upset because his grandmother, who lives far away, got sick and had to cancel her visit, reflect back his feelings to him, saying, "That is so disappointing. That would make me feel sad, too." This simple technique helps the child identify his feelings, reinforces the expression of feelings, and helps him connect feelings to thoughts and resulting behaviors. It also strengthens your relationship with the child as it demonstrates your understanding and compassion.

Step 3: Help Children Identify the Intensity of Their Feelings

As we have seen, children with autism commonly go from "zero to sixty" in experiencing their feelings. They tend to experience the world in concrete, black or white ways so that they feel either happy or sad. By helping children identify the intensity of their feelings, they can better regulate their emotions and engage in coping strategies.

The use of a ratings scale helps children register different degrees of emotion so that they can determine if they need to engage in a coping strategy. For example, on Kari Dunn Buron's "incredible five-point scale" (2012), each of the five points represents a different level of intensity for a particular feeling (see appendix). The following example usefully applies to anger, an emotion frequently expressed in an overreactive manner:

When teaching about feelings, show children how to

1. **define feelings;**
2. **identify feelings;**
3. **identify the intensity of their feelings; and**
4. **use coping skills.**

1. Annoyed
2. A little upset
3. Angry
4. Really Mad
5. Furious

Children can describe an event related to each feeling to show that different circumstances lead to emotional reactions of varying levels. A similar tool for helping children identify the intensity of their feelings is a "feelings thermometer." Using a picture of a thermometer to describe a single emotion, we can have children fill in different "degrees" of a feeling, with higher levels, written in red, indicating greater intensity (see appendix). After introducing the ratings scale or feelings thermometer, we should make sure to refer to these tools in our daily routines to help children become fluent in identifying the feelings that apply to them in a given moment.

Step 4: Teach Coping Skills

Teach coping skills so that children know what to do when they experience intense feelings. We can offer explicit instruction on coping skills, making sure that children practice these skills when they are regulated so that they will have experience with these techniques before they need to access them when they are upset. Coping skills can be as straightforward as taking a break, which is a quick, simple, and portable intervention. Other techniques can be a bit more involved. For example, teach the child "the turtle" by having him cross his arms in front of him and put his head down. This position represents the child going into his shell to stop, think, and calm down.

PRACTICE COPING SKILLS

Because children cannot attain self-regulation if they do not know how to cope with difficult feelings and situations, it is important to practice a variety of techniques that anyone can use for calming down and managing strong emotions. We can teach children specific movements, responses, and actions that function to redirect thought processes and interrupt the downward spiral into overwhelming anxiety, anger, or other intense feelings. Below we offer some examples of concrete coping skills we can teach children. These coping skills are especially useful because children can enact most of them on their own in almost any place.

1. *Take three deep breaths.* This intervention takes just a few seconds and is sometimes just the pause that the child needs to process his thoughts and connect his thoughts to emotions.
2. *Counting.* This strategy is similar in that it also takes just a few seconds and offers the child time to process a difficult or stressful experience. The rhythm and predictability of counting promotes self-regulation and calming. Counting can be accompanied by tapping, perhaps lightly on one's knees, to increase sensory input.
3. *Squeeze hands together tightly.* This is also referred to as "peanut butter jelly hands." Instruct the children to pretend to spread peanut

butter on one palm and jelly on the other palm. Then, they should squeeze their palms together as tightly as they can. This is an effective coping skill, particularly for children who have difficulty keeping their hands to themselves or those who need a physical outlet to express their anger. The squeezing motion of the hands provides pressure and sensory input that may help to calm the child. It's very easy to give this visual cue to children who need to engage in this technique: simply squeeze your own hands together.

4. *Verbalize your feelings.* The goal of this strategy is for the child to tell someone how he is feeling. For example, teach the child to use his words by saying, "I'm mad." Because autistic children, as we have seen, frequently have difficulty verbalizing their feelings, it's helpful to model this technique and incorporate it into the daily routine whenever appropriate.

5. *Ask for help.* Autistic children also often have difficulty asking for help, because doing so represents a loss of control and lack of ability. Encourage asking for help by reflecting to the child, "It looks like you might like some help." Also model how to ask for help by using the words, "I need help, please," as you approach to offer assistance. Reinforce this behavior by rewarding children when they seek the support of the adult. Give the child a visual cue card that represents "help" in case the child finds it easier to use a signal than to verbalize his needs.

Teaching children how to enact these coping skills and offering them explicit instruction about feelings are key strategies for strengthening their capacity for self-regulation. As this chapter also suggests, we increase a child's ability to self-regulate when we model empathy and practice problem-solving skills ourselves. Our very interactions with a child become perhaps the most powerful platform for teaching skills of self-regulation when we commit to the following course of action:

- taking time to understand a child's perspective before reacting;
- appealing to reason and seeking the child's input in solving a problem; and
- offering the child opportunities to make choices based on his awareness of his own needs and interests.

As we saw earlier with Raymond, who initially refused to put on his bathing suit, taking the time to elicit and understand his perspective was crucial in helping Raymond address his needs and solve a problem. Anytime that we can acknowledge a child's point of view and demonstrate that we understand the reasons behind it, we help him grow emotionally by modeling sensitivity and showing the value of putting feelings into language. We also provide opportunities for his emotional intelligence to grow by involving him, whenever possible, in the decisions that affect him. Having a sense of agency helps the child see the connections among his actions in the world and his emotional experiences.

Overall, we want to support children in becoming aware of their feelings and recognizing the events or circumstances that cause them to have strong reactions. And, ultimately, we want children to be able to enact strategies that allow them to maintain emotional control or return to a state of self-regulation. We must remember, however, that this is the *end goal*. There will be bumps and setbacks along the way. It is for this reason that we must consider the best way to manage times of dysregulation and challenging behavior.

WHEN ALL ELSE FAILS: WHAT TO DO DURING A MELTDOWN

Despite our best efforts at employing strategies and using tools to promote self-regulation, sometimes autistic children become dysregulated and have a meltdown. During a meltdown, they might engage in a range of extreme behavior that can include screaming, yelling, crying, cursing, name calling, hitting, biting, and throwing objects. Such behavior can be scary for all involved, and it can cause bystanders to become dysregulated, upsetting children and adults alike.

Temper Tantrums vs. Meltdowns

It can be difficult to distinguish between a temper tantrum and a meltdown because both involve extreme behaviors such as hitting, kicking, biting, and screaming. However, it's important to understand the differences between these two types of episodes because when an autistic child is experiencing a meltdown, ordinary behavioral approaches intended for temper tantrums are often not effective.

Temper Tantrum	Meltdown
• Aimed at a specific goal	• Not goal oriented
• Child maintains a sense of control over herself	• Child has no control over behavior and emotions
• Child pays attention to the reactions of others	• Child is unconcerned with other people's reactions
• Ends rather quickly when goal is attained	• Lasts a long time and ends only after it has run its course

Develop a "Crisis" Plan

The key to dealing with a meltdown is to have a plan in place and enact the plan when needed. This is commonly called a crisis plan. Though this phrase has a negative connotation, it's nonetheless relevant because a crisis represents a situation of instability or emotional upheaval. Although a crisis plan should be individualized to meet a child's specific needs, there are some key points that should always be included:

1. *Protect the child, other children, and adults to keep people safe.* If the child is in danger of hurting himself or others by, for example, hurling a laptop across the room, it may be necessary to remove the child from the area. For small children (ages three to five), two adults can quickly walk a child out of the room, leading her into a safe place that previously has been designated for crises. Ideally, this would be a relatively small room with mats on the floor and little equipment in it. In cases when a child is in imminent danger of hurting himself or others, it may be necessary to physically restrain the child, an act that requires specialized training and that should be used only as a last resort.

2. *Allow the child to calm down by himself if this is deemed a safe and viable option.* The child can go to a quiet place to calm down in the home or classroom if it's not too disruptive. Or he can go to a previously designated location at home or school.

3. *Give the child as little attention as possible during a meltdown.* It's important to avoid rewarding this behavior with attention, even if it's negative attention. Let the child know that he can rejoin the family or class activity as soon as he is calm, but otherwise say little. Talking to the child can be perceived as attention and may lengthen the meltdown.

4. *Once the child has calmed down, reinforce positive behavior.* Praise the child for having a calm body. Ask the child if she is ready to return to the home or classroom activity.

5. *Preview the expectations for returning to the activity.* For example, tell the child that she needs to have a calm body and keep hands and feet to herself.

Tailor the crisis plan to address the child's individual needs: make note of particular triggers, provide objects or toys that promote calming, offer effective forms of sensory input, and list specific words or mantras that are soothing. Once an autistic child has experienced the strong emotions involved in a meltdown, it's sometimes difficult for her to return to a state of regulation. Be prepared to offer additional support to help the child cope. Although the upheaval of a meltdown is difficult and disruptive for everyone, remember that it's most traumatic for the child herself.

Five-year-old Maya, for example, becomes angry and aggressive, and it's not clear why she gets so upset. She throws objects across the room; she yells, cries, curses, and screams, "I hate you," when adults approach to help her. Two younger children are also present in the room. The adults quickly remove these other children (Step 1: protect other children), and they ask Maya what's wrong. She is unable to answer and throws more objects. It's clear that Maya needs a safe place to calm down because she is being too destructive to remain where she is, and any attempts to help her only seem to escalate her behavior.

The two adults quickly approach Maya. Each person places one hand under her arm and one hand on the outside of her shoulder, and they guide her swiftly to her previously designated safety spot, an unoccupied room down the hall (Step 2: allow the child to calm down in a safe space). This setting, as should be the case in any crisis plan, is not a punitive environment. Parents and teachers should never seclude a child in a small, dark room or confine her within a space that seems threatening. Though the idea is to escort the child to an area where she can't damage property or hurt other people, the overarching goal is to de-escalate the situation and help the child calm down—something that cannot be accomplished if the child feels unsafe or intimidated by the adults around her.

Once Maya is in her safe space, the adults tell her that she can join the others again when she is calm. The adults stay nearby but they don't engage with Maya, and out of their peripheral vision they see her kicking the wall while she cries for several minutes. (Step 3: provide as little attention as possible); then it is quiet. After a few minutes of silence, they tell Maya that she can leave the safety spot when she is ready. Maya chooses to stay by herself for several more minutes, then she approaches the adults. The adults praise her for calming down (Step 4: reinforce positive behavior) and tell her that she can return to be with the other people once she picks up the objects she threw (Step 5: preview the expectations for returning to the activity). They ask Maya to talk about what happened when she is ready. After listening carefully to her, the adults help Maya identify the trigger for her extreme behavior. They then brainstorm different ways to solve the problem next time. More importantly, they make a proactive plan to prevent it from occurring in the first place.

THE TAKEAWAY

As parents and teachers, we need to support autistic children in their efforts to do well by employing a range of strategies that make those efforts pay off. To this end, there are practical techniques we can incorporate and simple accommodations we can make so that our classrooms and homes become environments that foster children's ability to self-regulate. The preceding chapters outline how we can set children up for success by offering a plan that is comprehensive yet also straightforward and easy to implement.

Adjust Learning Experiences and the Environment	*Emphasize Structure and Consistency*	*Foster Collaboration and Emotional Awareness*
• Use pictures • Facilitate planning and organization • Offer incentives and rewards	• Create a visual schedule • Engage in previewing • Anticipate transitions and build in breaks	• Offer choices • Solve problems together • Teach about feelings and coping skills

All of these strategies work in different ways not only to reduce the anxiety that autistic children so often experience, but to offer support and targeted instruction ultimately aimed at building skills of self-regulation. Whether we adjust the physical environment of our home or classrooms, approach problems collaboratively, preview the daily schedule, or teach lessons about feelings, we are working proactively to set children up for success by creating a coherent system of support that nurtures a child's capacity for self-regulation. And in the unavoidable instances when an autistic child becomes dysregulated and has a meltdown, we still have a plan in place that prevents a temporary setback from undermining the path to success.

Even these challenging episodes become a key part of emotional growth when we help children learn that they can make it through difficult situations, move forward after mistakes, and regroup in the wake of painful feelings. All these abilities are at the core of self-regulation—the skill necessary for both making it through the day and facing future challenges with resilience.

III

SOCIAL SKILLS

"I wish I knew how to play with those kids."
"I never know what to do or what to say. What's wrong with me?"
"Those kids are always playing together, and I'm left out."
"Other kids are laughing, and I don't know why. What's so funny?"
"Why am I so different?"

These statements, spoken by young autistic children, reveal the impact of their struggles with social skills. As their own words attest, these children feel alienated, bewildered, and anxious. The social world feels overwhelming and intimidating to them, and their interactions with other people are all too often chaotic and confusing. Although autistic children may be highly articulate and eager to make friends, they do not always instinctively understand how to engage with others. They need help learning to navigate the complicated social world (Attwood, 2007).

Social interactions are complex for all people, whether they have autism or not. Even the briefest exchange with another person is a multilayered and dynamic act. Not only do we engage in conversation during a social interaction, but we process information from emotional cues, social contexts, and other forms of nonverbal communication (Quill, 2000). In an exchange with a person we know or recently have met, we also remember and apply relevant historical contexts such as previous conversations and recollections of the other person's likes and dislikes. Let's examine the following conversation as an example of this complexity.

John: "Hey, Sam. Do you want to play Legos with me?"

Sam: "I can't right now. I'm doing this puzzle."

John: "Can I help you with it?"

Sam: "Sure."

In this scenario, before John even asks Sam to play, we can see that he first remembers that Sam likes Legos. John is also able to adjust his expectations quickly when he recognizes that Sam is busy working on a puzzle. He reads Sam's body language, which affirms that he is engrossed in the activity, and he comes to understand that Sam wants to finish the puzzle. In this moment, John considers Sam's wishes and needs; he sees the situation from Sam's perspective. John then recalls that Sam is very good at puzzles, and he thinks that it might be fun to join him. Here, John once again considers Sam's perspective and asks if he can work on the puzzle, too. Throughout this short conversation, John's communication is flexible, reciprocal, and engaging.

However, these are attributes that often do not come readily to autistic children (Quill, 2000). In fact, deficits in social skills are one of the primary diagnostic criteria for children on the autism spectrum. The social challenges affecting autistic children have potentially serious consequences for their well-being, both in daily life and in the long term. In addition to being misperceived as selfish or aloof, autistic children struggle with powerful emotions that arise from an awareness of their own social challenges.

They feel anxious and confused.
They feel they can't understand others.
They feel left out and alienated.
They feel different and incompetent.
They feel overwhelmed in social situations.

These emotions impair the development of children's self-esteem, and they make it virtually impossible for them to achieve self-regulation. How can autistic children feel "just right" in a world where they struggle to understand the thoughts, motivations, and feelings of others? How can they feel at ease when social interaction doesn't seem meaningful or fulfilling?

In classrooms and other social settings, children with autism are often seen sitting alone or doing things by themselves while their peers are engaged and interacting with one another. It is a common misconception that such children want to be by themselves. They simply lack the skills for interacting successfully with others. The following chapters offer strategies aimed at mitigating the social challenges associated with autism. We first discuss what these challenges are and how they affect a child's ability to self-regulate and function on a daily basis. We then outline techniques that parents and teachers can use to help children gain the necessary skills to feel successful in their relations with other people.

6

AUTISTIC CHILDREN AND SOCIAL SKILLS CHALLENGES

Whereas neurotypical children generally learn social conventions by observing others, autistic children often need to be taught these conventions explicitly. With such teaching, they can ultimately build a repertoire of rules and skills to apply to social situations (Attwood, 2007). Before we discuss the specific strategies for teaching social skills, however, it's first important to understand why autistic children struggle with forms of interaction that seem almost effortless for their neurotypical peers.

By the age of four most children have mastered an array of social skills. They can read a person's body language and facial expressions and infer meaning from these nonverbal cues. They usually show sensitivity to others' feelings, often making connections between specific emotions and behaviors. They can also read environmental cues and easily imitate other people.

In general, neurotypical children are able to link new experiences to past experiences as they remember meaningful social data and use that information in subsequent exchanges. In a similar way, they can make generalizations from a specific situation, applying their knowledge from one experience to other relevant contexts. During social interactions, most neurotypical children process information from multiple sources. They instinctively filter out irrelevant distractions, shifting their attention to what is important. These skills, however, do not come as readily for most autistic children, and we now highlight some of the social challenges that they face.

THEORY OF MIND: WHAT'S IN YOUR MIND
IS DIFFERENT FROM WHAT'S IN MY MIND

One of the most prominent social difficulties that autistic children experience involves theory of mind, which refers to a person's ability to understand the perspectives and intentions of others. When John, in the opening to part III, recognizes that Sam wants to continue building his puzzle instead of playing Legos, he exercises theory of mind. This ability allows children to comprehend social behaviors, predict what others might do, and surmise what others are thinking and feeling. Based on this awareness of another's perspective, children are able to adjust their own behavior and emotional expression (Quill, 2000).

Let's look at another brief example of a child exercising theory of mind. Three-year-old Lily asks Griffin if he would like to play freeze tag with her, but Griffin does not answer and returns his attention to the stack of blocks he's been building. Lily observes this nonverbal behavior and predicts that Griffin does not want to leave his blocks to play tag. She then emphasizes to Griffin how much fun tag will be, telling him that he can play with the blocks later and that she will play blocks with him then.

In this case, Lily adjusts her behavior based on her thoughts about what Griffin might be thinking. She tries to make playing tag even more enticing, and she offers to play blocks with him in return, demonstrating reciprocity. Lily's social instincts ultimately pay off as she successfully persuades Griffin that her plan will be fun. The two of them head off to play tag, saving the blocks for later.

For children on the autism spectrum, however, social exchanges rarely happen with such ease. One reason for this difficulty is that autistic people seem to have impaired neural connections in the parts of the brain responsible for social skills and language (Hua et al., 2011). These weakened connections compromise a person's ability to process facial expressions and understand the relationship between himself and the environment (Cheng et al., 2015). In a typically functioning neurological system, "mirror" neurons enable a person to replicate or mimic other people and to experience cognitive empathy, the ability to see things from another person's perspective (Frith & Frith, 2009; Leslie et al., 2004). But in individuals with autism, mirror neurons do not seem to fire correctly. This neurodifference affects the capacity for cognitive empathy, often making it difficult for autistic people to seek out social interaction, relate to other people, and learn from others' behavior (Dapretto et al., 2006). It is important to emphasize, however, that these challenges do not interfere with an autistic person's capacity for emotional or affective empathy, which allows us to feel the same emotions that other people feel and to experience compassion and genuine concern for others (Jones et al., 2010). In some cases, autistic people seem to be more sensitive to other people's feelings, absorbing the distress or calmness experienced by those around them.

Autistic people, then, often have high levels of affective or emotional empathy while also struggling with cognitive empathy and theory of mind. People with autism readily share in the emotional experiences of others even as they have trouble with the cognitive acts of reading body language, facial expression, and other social cues to interpret another person's thoughts and intentions (Attwood,

> **The idea that autistic people do not feel empathy is a myth. Though they may struggle with perspective taking, they feel other people's emotions and experience compassion just as neurotypicals do.**

2007). These challenges can make it especially hard for autistic children to infer meaning from social interactions (Winner, 2007). They can sense another person's feelings, and they can be profoundly moved by those feelings, but they have difficulty interpreting emotions and seeing things from the other person's point of view (Nason, 2014). They frequently think that everyone else is thinking about the same thing they are—that their perspective and opinions are shared by everyone (Frith & de Vignemont, 2005).

When people do not understand how neurological differences affect an autistic child's social skills, they can misinterpret the child's behavior and mannerisms all too easily. In some cases, for example, autistic children may be perceived as aloof or disrespectful because they appear to be ignoring someone when they have simply missed the social cues that seem obvious to neurotypical people (Attwood, 2007).

Autistic children also might appear to be rude because they can be brutally honest at times. It is not uncommon for autistic children to point out other people's mistakes or tell others exactly what they think without first considering the potential effects of their words. For example, an autistic child might say, "I don't like your shirt," or "You have brown spots on your arms." They have not yet developed awareness of social norms such as telling white lies or keeping critical comments to themselves in order to be polite. From their perspective, they are simply stating the obvious. On the positive side, the extreme honesty of autistic children means that we usually can count on them to tell the truth. If a child has done something wrong, he is likely to own up to his actions and admit to whatever mistakes he has made.

Because autistic children struggle with theory of mind, peer interactions can be challenging. One example of such difficulty can be seen in the tendency of autistic children to misperceive accidental situations as intentional acts. For example, five-year-old Rachel gets mad at David for bumping into her and elbowing her in the arm. Even though David immediately apologizes and explains that it was an accident, Rachel can see the encounter only from her perspective: David bumped into her arm and it really hurts. She does not consider the situation from David's viewpoint, recognizing that David tripped and lost his balance. Because autistic children like Rachel can have difficulty recognizing other people's intentions, they may feel an increased sense of paranoia, believing that some acts are purposeful when they're not (Attwood, 2007).

Challenges with theory of mind also make it hard for children to play with their peers and manage conflicts when they arise. Autistic children often adhere strongly to their point of view—the one they instinctively recognize (Attwood, 2007). An autistic child, for example, may have his own ideas about how games should be played, and he expects everyone to follow suit. When a disagreement inevitably ensues, he also has trouble negotiating and prioritizing the needs of others because his viewpoint overshadows everyone else's perspective. For example, it is not uncommon for an autistic child to refuse to apologize to someone because the child does not readily understand that he has hurt the other person's feelings.

"You know why I'm upset because you know what I'm thinking," said a young girl with limited theory of mind.

Although an autistic child may appear to be bossy or stubborn in such situations, we should be aware that his desire for control stems from his challenges with theory of mind. Because autistic children often have trouble recognizing other people's priorities, feelings, and reasoning, it is not easy for them to incorporate others' ideas into their social interactions or play schemes (Attwood, 2007). Their rigidity in this regard can make everyone frustrated.

Neurotypical children can become disenchanted with an autistic child's lack of flexibility quickly. As a result, the autistic child himself may ultimately find it easier to give up on peer relations, choosing to spend time alone because it feels impossible to make friends. In struggling with theory of mind, then, autistic children potentially experience significant frustration themselves.

Think about how they perceive the world. If you believe that everyone else thinks the same thing that you do, then it is confusing and distressing when people do not behave in the ways you expect. Challenges with theory of mind thus clearly interfere with a child's capacity to self-regulate. An autistic child's rigidity stems not only from the tendency to prioritize his own perspective, but from the emotional difficulty that arises as he reacts to the unsettling and unpredictable actions of other people.

EGOCENTRISM: IT'S ALL ABOUT ME

Autism comes from the Greek word *autos*, meaning "self." One of the defining features of autism is being self-focused or "egocentric." Not to be confused with the term "egotistical," which has negative connotations of "selfishness," egocentrism is a psychological term that simply describes a focus on the self. Just as autistic people struggle with theory of mind, they also tend to be interested in their own likes and desires, seemingly to the point of being unaware of others' interests, needs, and wants. They may have a tendency to prioritize their own perspectives, talk about themselves, and assume that everyone else is interested in their ideas.

This intense self-focus makes it hard for many autistic children to successfully engage in conversations or other social interactions. At times, they can try to control social situations and tell other people what to do. In such instances, they seek to make social interactions—which are often unpredictable—conform to their ideas and viewpoints. Attempting to control a situation by being overly directive is a way of trying to have their needs met and reduce their anxiety.

NONVERBAL COMMUNICATION DOESN'T COMMUNICATE

During a typical conversation, we not only listen to what another person is saying, but we also take in a great deal of information that is not spoken. Often without even realizing it, we pay attention to the other person's body language, voice intonation, and facial expressions. We rely on these nonverbal cues to make inferences about the other person's emotions, thoughts, and intentions. The ability to draw meaning from these other aspects of a conversation is crucial because more information is ultimately conveyed through nonverbal communication than through verbal communication (Nason, 2014).

Neurotypical children usually can understand nonverbal cues instinctively. As early as infancy, babies learn to get their parents' attention and maintain reciprocal interaction (Quill, 2000). By preschool age, it is evident that most children can adjust their conversation and behavior based on their recognition of another person's eye gaze, body movement, voice intonation, and gestures (Quill, 2000). Neurotypical preschoolers usually can recognize the subtleties of facial expression and make a happy, angry, or scared face upon request.

However, autistic children frequently do not register these forms of nonverbal communication, and they are unable to adjust their own communication style in response to important social cues, such as someone looking away to indicate boredom. Whereas most neurotypical four-year-olds can make inferences based on the eye gaze of others, children on the autism spectrum usually have trouble making eye contact, and they are more likely to look at the speaker's mouth (Baron-Cohen, 2001; Rutishauser et al., 2013). Some autistic people have described looking into people's eyes as a painful or uncomfortable experience (Grandin, 1995). Recent studies also suggest that autistic children may not look at other people who are speaking because they are concentrating on the content of their words (Jaswal & Akhtar, 2018). There are adverse social effects of decreased eye contact, however, and many autistic children miss out on the information conveyed through a person's eyes, an important resource for interpreting another's thoughts and feelings.

Understanding the concept of personal space is also frequently elusive for children with autism. Whereas most neurotypical children intuitively recognize how to position their bodies in relation to other people, autistic children can have trouble recognizing appropriate physical boundaries. In social situations, they sometimes stand too far away from the people they are interacting with, or at other times they may be too physically intrusive. For example, one three-year-old autistic boy often touched people's hair, legs, arms, and shoulders. He occasionally even licked other people, yet he didn't recognize when others winced in response to these actions. He also didn't understand that his behavior influenced how other children felt about him and behaved toward him.

CONVERSATIONS ARE A QUANDARY

Conversations can be especially challenging for autistic children because they necessitate that the speaker and listener be in tune with one another so as to understand the other's interests and intentions. For a conversation to go smoothly, then, both parties must possess theory of mind. Each person must take turns talking so that both people have an equal opportunity to share information and ideas. Ideally, the speaker also accommodates his topic of conversation to the listener's interests, and the listener remains attentive to the different forms of communication at play. This includes both spoken language and the nonverbal cues that convey emotional information about the speaker and his probable intentions. In short, conversations are complex, reciprocal, and constantly changing.

Lots of people, including many with autism, struggle with conversational skills for multiple reasons. Some autistic children, for example, find it especially hard to initiate conversations and social interactions (Winner, 2007). They frequently want to get involved and talk with others, but they shy away from doing so because they feel insecure and uncomfortable. Sometimes autistic people struggle with conversations because they can be overly focused on what they want to say without paying attention to the other person or monitoring the relevance of the conversation to the listener's interests (Quill, 2000). When people with autism struggle with reciprocal communication in this way, they seek to limit conversations to a topic in which they have some mastery or expertise. By engaging in such "monologues," autistic people often attempt to manage the unpredictability that's intrinsic to any back-and-forth conversation (Prizant, 2015).

For example, Sean is a five-year-old boy who adores *Star Wars*. Bolstered by a prodigious memory and eye for detail, he talks on and on about *Star Wars*, recounting the plots of multiple films in their entirety. He speaks in a monotone voice and turns his body away from the listener, never looking at the listener's eyes and rarely looking at his face. Sean discusses his favorite topic without ever noticing if the listener understands or cares about the intricate *Star Wars* plot details. Eventually, the listener stops paying attention, but Sean seems unaware of this development and continues speaking.

Children on the autism spectrum also often have difficulty interpreting figurative speech, which requires the listener to understand the speaker's intent and to read between the lines. There is a tendency among autistic children to take language literally, and it is not uncommon for them to misunderstand metaphors, jokes, sarcasm, and idioms. For example, a child might be troubled upon hearing his father say "My head is killing me" because he thinks that his father actually might die. Another child might interpret an instance of exaggeration literally. Hearing his mother say "We'll never get to grandma's house," the child thinks they'll really *never* reach their destination.

COGNITIVE PROCESSING

As we have seen, social interactions require multiple levels of processing. When we talk with others, we must remember relevant contextual information, interpret nonverbal information such as body language, and coordinate communication in a reciprocal way. Neurotypical people, especially those with polished social skills, can readily process information from these multiple sources, filtering out irrelevant details and shifting their attention to important social and emotional cues. They can therefore remember meaningful social data and use it in future encounters with people, making generalizations about how to interact with others. But it can be challenging for people with autism to master these skills because they process information differently. Interpreting multiple messages or data at once can prove to be overwhelming as this skill involves different neural pathways in the brain that may be impaired in autistic children (Nason, 2014).

In addition, people on the autism spectrum tend to process information intellectually, viewing their interactions with others in a more cerebral way. They often perceive the content or subject matter of a conversation as the most meaningful aspect of a social interaction. While nearly everyone enjoys relationships with people who share similar interests, children with autism more frequently prioritize relationships with people who care about the matters that interest them most.

Autistic people also often have a remarkable capacity for remembering numerous facts and details, and this skill affects their social interactions. Sometimes the details of an event stand out to a person with autism, overshadowing the wider significance of a social experience (Nason, 2014). For example, after attending a birthday party, Sarah remembers the color of the icing on the cake, a large pimple on someone's nose, and the grades on a report card hanging on the fridge. However, she seems to lack awareness of the bigger picture. The party's larger meaning as a social experience is less significant for Sarah, and she does not have a strong impression of the birthday boy being happy and having fun with everyone who came to celebrate his special day. These differences in processing and remembering information greatly affect the relationships people have.

People on the autism spectrum may feel out of sync with neurotypical people and vice versa. In particular, autistic children may not understand why neurotypicals do not seem as interested in their preferred topics. They may feel perplexed by the ways that other people try to relate to them. They may come to view neurotypical people as overly emotional, confusing, or perhaps even stupid (Grandin, 2013).

INCREASED ANXIETY

Imagine that you land on a foreign planet, not understanding how its inhabitants communicate, but you desperately want to get to know them. After many attempts to make a connection, you still don't understand why these people act the way they do. There seems to be a set of rules for communicating that is incomprehensible to you, and the other people don't seem to understand you, either. This is a common experience for children on the autism spectrum. Their unsuccessful attempts to communicate create feelings of inadequacy and impede the development of positive self-esteem. They become more anxious about trying to interact with people. This anxiety, in turn, decreases their motivation and desire to socialize.

Feelings of inadequacy, incompetence, and worry therefore undermine their attempts to reach out to others. Often, such children desperately want to be involved in social activities but do not know how to initiate personal interactions. We must not mistake their avoidance for a lack of interest in engaging with others. One autistic girl explains this predicament succinctly: "I really want to talk to those kids, but I don't know how."

Common Social Skills Challenges

Autistic children may:

- Confuse other people's perspectives with their own
- Find body language and facial expressions puzzling
- Prioritize their own interests in conversation and play
- Struggle to differentiate meaningful information from irrelevant details
- Initiate social exchanges abruptly or unconventionally
- Intrude on others' personal space
- Show rigidity and seek to control the unpredictability of social interaction

---

HOW KIDS TRY TO COPE WITH THESE CHALLENGES

Children on the autism spectrum are often highly intelligent and recognize that they are different from their neurotypical peers. They may have a variety of responses to feeling different, alienated, and overwhelmed. Some children, for example, internalize these feelings of inadequacy and become depressed. Others use their intellect to compensate for poor social skills and become "little professors," lecturing to others about their favorite topics.

Some use escapist fantasies to deal with social anxiety, creating their own world of pretend friends. In other cases, autistic children may attempt to learn social skills by mimicking their friends in the privacy of their own homes and then practicing on their peers. Still others externalize their feelings of inadequacy so that their anxiety manifests as anger projected outward at others. Everyone else has a problem, not them. These children can appear to be insensitive or even defiant as they blame others for social conflict and often resist being corrected.

Hal is a five-year-old autistic boy who employs many of these strategies in an attempt to manage the uncertainty he feels in the realm of social interaction. Turning to a topic on which he is an expert, Hal brings up Disney movies whenever he talks to other people. He derives self-confidence from his vast knowledge of Disney films, and he uses his interest to "teach" his friends intricate details about the movies and how they were made. At times, he attempts to make conversation by trying out portions of dialogue he's memorized from the films. Yet this deep knowledge of Disney movies and the self-assurance it brings him doesn't improve Hal's social interactions, for his attempts at conversation turn into monologues. He doesn't notice that others become disinterested and walk away.

Because Hal feels happy thinking about his favorite Disney films, he continues talking about them to himself. At home, he develops a fantasy world, imagining that he has friends with whom to share his stories. This activity allows him to escape from the anxiety and stress of social situations. He practices conversations he has heard in the movies, but the people he speaks with exist only in his imagination. None of these strategies is effective in helping Hal learn social skills. He remains alienated from his peers, he continues to feel different and inadequate when around other people, and he does not progress in learning how to make friends.

We now turn our attention to strategies that are effective in helping children like Hal learn social skills.

7

TEACHING SOCIAL THINKING

Just as visitors to a foreign country can benefit from a guide to help them understand different language and customs, autistic children can benefit from instruction that helps them become familiar with the unwritten social code that structures much human interaction. As parents and teachers, it is our job to make this terrain feel less foreign not only by teaching social skills, but also by developing a connection with autistic children and engaging with them in ways that spark their interest.

We must first reach out to children so that they know we are interested in them as individuals and that we care about what they have to say. Preschools and day cares are particularly good environments for supporting a child's social growth because these settings allow for the development of sustained relationships with children, and they are places that are structured by clear rules and expectations. There is a schedule for the day that is largely predictable and a consistent set of people with whom a child interacts. This sense of routine and familiarity helps autistic children feel safe and secure even as we encourage them to stretch and make social gains. These learning environments also include neurotypical children who can serve as models for children on the spectrum. It helps if autistic children have regular interaction with their neurotypical peers so that they have opportunities for communicating and playing with them (Attwood, 2007).

One of the most important ways to strengthen the social skills of children on the autism spectrum is to teach them "social thinking" (Winner, 2007). This term, which is closely related to theory of mind, refers to being aware of what others are thinking, making interpretations of social experiences, and incorporating this information into one's interactions with other people. Social thinking is of crucial importance because a successful relationship or personal exchange depends on being able to

65

have at least some recognition of another person's motivations, opinions, personality traits, and emotions.

In this chapter, we offer techniques to build social thinking that are easy to incorporate into a child's daily routines and habits. Some of these are formal activities that teachers can use with the whole class or a group of students. Parents can also try these out with their children at home. Other strategies are more spontaneous, and parents and teachers can weave these techniques into a child's daily life, working to facilitate positive social interactions when opportunities arise.

Although all these strategies are aimed at helping children with social skills challenges, they will certainly benefit neurotypical peers and siblings as well. After all, most children (and even some adults) can use a little extra help when it comes to thinking about other people's feelings and engaging cooperatively with their peers. Let's turn now to explore effective strategies for teaching social thinking,

ESTABLISH RULES

One strategy for teaching children to engage in social thinking is to develop a list of rules for interacting with others. These rules are not meant to be a list of prohibitive behaviors; rather they are designed to function as a guide that gives children a specific framework for social experiences that often feel chaotic and overwhelming to them. Because autistic children tend to be more concrete thinkers, they often respond well to clear and concise rules.

Specific social rules can be reviewed with children immediately before playing a game, and more general social rules can be reviewed prior to a social interaction or at the start of the day. Mantras can also be developed from social rules for children to repeat to themselves to remind them of social expectations.

Below we offer a few rules that are essential in developing social thinking. These are hidden or unwritten social codes that need to be made evident and explained to children in a clear and concrete manner, being specific about what to say and what not to say.

Rule #1: What's in My Head Is Not What's in Your Head

This rule helps to establish theory of mind, the foundation for developing other important social skills. We can reinforce this rule by demonstrating in a variety of ways that what the child is thinking differs from what other people are thinking. Here are two examples of activities that help promote theory of mind:

- *Play guessing games.* Look at someone's face and guess what he might be thinking. For example, say, "Look at your brother. What do you think he's thinking right now after you took his toy away from him?" This guessing game helps children pay attention to facial expressions and interpret them. It also helps children recognize in a concrete way that other people have thoughts and perspectives that are different from their own.
- *Discuss opinions.* Point out how people have different opinions because they think differently about the same topics. Build the notion of opinions into everyday conversations about television shows, movies, toys, colors, weather, and so forth. Emphasize that it is natural and okay for people to have different opinions. If a child blurts out that his friend Rhys got an ugly haircut, point out that Rhys probably thinks something different about how his hair looks.

Rule #2: All People Have Thoughts about Others

This rule helps to teach children with autism that other people are thinking about them, just as they themselves have thoughts about other people (Winner, 2007). Integrate this concept into the child's daily routine. For example, when the autistic child shares a toy with a friend, ask him, "What is your friend thinking about you now that you've shared with him? Do you think he thinks you are kind and a good friend? Do you think he will want to play with you again when you are kind to him?" This is an important rule because it teaches children not only about social thinking, but that people's thoughts about you influence their behavior toward you.

In addition, it's important for autistic children to understand that not all of their thoughts about others should be verbalized. When explaining what they should not say, be specific. For example, tell them not to comment on how people look unless they have something nice to tell others. This is a concrete yet hidden rule that must be taught, especially because autistic children sometimes don't see a problem with reporting a truthful statement and announcing that someone is fat or old, for example. We all have thoughts about others, and others have thoughts about us, but we don't say everything that we are thinking out loud.

Rule #3: Most People Don't Want You to Touch Them

This is an important rule because many children with autism have poor social boundaries. Other people may distance themselves from children who, for example, touch those around them as a misguided way of initiating social interaction or of showing excitement. Some autistic children may also hit or squeeze someone out of frustration or anxiety. This rule helps children learn about personal boundaries, and it also reinforces the idea that just because the child wants something doesn't mean the other person wants it, too. So as not to discourage acceptable forms of affection, teach this rule with the following caveat: if you want to touch someone, ask them first. Moreover, touching mom or dad may be an appropriate exception to this rule.

Rule #4: Everybody Wants to Have Fun

Because autistic children can be self-focused and sometimes seek to make play all about their needs, it is helpful to establish the rule that "everybody wants to have fun." By highlighting this rule prior to play, we can help children develop cooperative play skills and social thinking. Before starting a game, ask each child if he wants to have fun. When the kids say yes (because everyone likes to have a good time), call attention to their response and tell the group, "Okay, so everyone wants to have fun. Let's make sure this happens." Then turn to the child with autism in the group and say, "Would you help make sure that everyone has fun? I want you to be like an eagle, using your sharp eyes to make sure that everyone is having a good time. Will you be the eagle and be in charge of everyone having fun?"

Once the child agrees to play this role, ask him, "Would you check in with the kids in a few minutes and ask if everyone is enjoying the game? This way, we can be sure that everyone is having fun." Before moving on to the game, review the rules so everyone knows what to do to have a good time. While the kids are playing the game, turn to the "eagle" a few times, urging him to ask the others if they are having fun. If someone is not having a good time, then ask the children how they can solve the problem.

This strategy is valuable for all children because it teaches the whole group that concern for others is important. It also reinforces social thinking for autistic children by offering concrete ways to recognize when others are not having fun and to find a solution to that problem. This strategy also gives the child with autism a special job overseeing the game, which helps him feel more secure and fulfills any need to be in control.

Parents and teachers can use a less formal version of this strategy in any scenario. Before a child begins playing with other kids, ask him, "Is this game just about you having fun or does everyone want to have fun?" Reinforce the value of thinking about others by reminding the child that "when everybody has fun, they will think it is fun to play with you and will want to play with you again."

LOOK, LISTEN, CLARIFY

Another means of encouraging social thinking is the "look, listen, clarify" technique, which describes how autistic children can learn to assess a social setting (Nason, 2014). Many children on the spectrum enter an unfamiliar social environment and find themselves unsure about how they should behave. This uncertainty leads to anxiety and increases the possibility of the child making a social blunder that may cause him to feel embarrassed. Teaching children these steps gives them a clear path about how to evaluate a new social situation and how to act based on their assessment of the environment:

- Step 1: *Look* around you and notice the social setting and context. What is going on here?
- Step 2: *Listen* to what is happening. Who's talking? What are they talking about?
- Step 3: *Clarify* what you should do. Should you join in quietly? Should you wait until the activity is done? What is the right thing to do for this social situation? Ask questions to find out what you should do.

Adults assisting the child in these steps can verbalize their observations to model this social thinking strategy. For example, a parent might say, "I'm noticing that the children are playing a game. It looks like there are teams. The children seem very excited about this game. Perhaps we can join this game, too. Do you want to ask the leader if we can join in?" This series of explicit observations describes the scene for the child, identifies the emotion in the scene, and offers problem-solving skills of how to be included in the game. As the child develops greater social awareness for himself, he will be better able to read the cues of a situation and make decisions based on this information.

SOCIAL STORIES

Social stories, developed by Carol Gray, are effective in previewing behavioral, social, and contextual expectations for a child. Many social stories lay the foundation of expected behavior, skills, or concepts for a given situation, building on the child's strengths. The story focuses on what a child should do, not what a child shouldn't do. There are many social stories available in books and on the internet (see appendix for resources on social stories). Social stories lend structure and predictability to a social context. They promote self-regulation in children by offering them a guide or road map that outlines a desired plan of action in response to certain events or situations.

> This is an example of a social story setting the expectation of being flexible when plans change.
>
> ### I Like Plan B
>
> I like to make a plan.
> I like to know what's happening.
> Sometimes our plans change. And that is okay.
> I might be expecting one thing, and then we have to make a change.
> We call this plan B.
> Plan B is when we can't do the first thing we planned.
> Instead we're going to do something else.
> It's cool to have a plan B.
> That way, we have another plan.
> I like plan B.

CREATE A SOCIAL FILE

Metaphors, with their use of concrete images, can be useful in teaching social skills to young children. For example, a parent or teacher can use a computer file or an actual file folder (depending on which the child understands better) to help a child learn to create a "social file" in his brain for each friend and relative he knows. You can explain this strategy by telling the child that it works like this:

> We keep information in files, and our brain can keep information on what we know about people too. We call these our "social files." Just as we have files for important papers, we also can keep files about our friends and family. We know that your friend Eric is allergic to chocolate

and that he loves to build things when playing. So the next time we see Eric, let's go get our social file about him and use the information in it to help us know what to do. Then we'll see that we shouldn't offer him any of our chocolate and that we should ask him if he wants to play Legos.

The information we keep in our social file is important in building relationships, especially friendships. We can access information in our social file anytime and use it to start conversations, engage, and play with others. We can help autistic children build their social files by reviewing what we know about different people, calling attention to what details we want to file away, and recognizing how this information may be useful in the future.

LITERATURE AND BATMAN

Literature and common media stories such as narratives about Batman or other superheroes can be used effectively to demonstrate social thinking and social skills (Attwood, 2007). While reading or telling a story, encourage social thinking by pausing to ask questions about a character's intentions, feelings, and perspectives. For example, you might say, "In this picture Batman looks mad. What do you think he's mad about? What do you think he'll do next?"

You might then turn to a picture of Robin, directing the child to look at this character's face. You could then ask, "Does Robin look as angry as Batman does? How do you think he feels? How can you tell?" In these examples, we ask children to try to understand someone else's perspective by encouraging them to look through the eyes of a fictional character who appeals to them.

Recognizing another person's perspective is a key element of social thinking, and all the strategies in this chapter seek to help children feel knowledgeable and confident in their interactions with others. Children cannot be self-regulated unless they understand the basic tenets of social engagement. We therefore want to support them in learning how to recognize other people's thoughts, evaluate new social situations, and engage in positive and meaningful interactions with others. And, as we have seen, there are practical tools for helping children develop these essential skills.

We can enumerate explicit rules for social interaction and offer them methods for assessing any social scene they may encounter. We can use concrete imagery, drawing on the notion of a social file to help children establish continuity and familiarity across discrete personal exchanges. Finally, we can turn to stories as a resource for building social thinking in autistic children. We can incorporate the specialized technique of the social story to lend structure to particular social situations, or we can weave lessons about intentions and perspectives into the stories we read for fun. These strategies for increasing social thinking greatly enrich a child's daily interactions. They also lay the groundwork for a child's mastery of the next social skill we discuss—having a conversation.

8

TEACHING CONVERSATIONAL SKILLS

Conversational skills are the basic building blocks of social interaction. It is virtually impossible to engage with other people successfully without possessing the ability to initiate and participate in reciprocal conversations. In this chapter we offer strategies that teach conversational skills to children on the spectrum who, as we have seen, often struggle with the unpredictable give-and-take of conversations.

WHOLE BODY LISTENING

Listening is a key component of conversational skills. "Whole body listening" is an important way to help children not only listen with their ears, but also to direct their faces, bodies, and minds toward the speaker (Winner, 2007). Encourage children to position their bodies (shoulders and torso) toward the listener and to look at the speaker's face when talking with other people. Acknowledge that some people feel uncomfortable looking at another person's eyes and tell children that they can look at the space between the person's eyebrows if that feels better to them. This instruction gives children a way to focus on people's faces without feeling anxious about having to make eye contact. Explain that faces give us a lot of information about people, including how they feel and what they might be thinking. Encourage the children to use their brains to think about what the speaker is saying. Also encourage the children to think of questions they want to ask that are related to the speaker's topic.

Playing charades is a fun way to help children focus on body language. Children can practice their whole body listening while being entertained as others act out concepts and ideas. Charades emphasizes the importance of body language in a concrete way by foregrounding how it gives us essential information. In one version of the game, ask a child to make different facial expressions and have the other children guess what that person is feeling or thinking. This game also encourages social thinking and enables children to practice interpreting others' intentions and emotions.

A CONVERSATION IS LIKE A TENNIS GAME

This strategy helps children conceptualize the reciprocal nature of a conversation. Explain to children that conversations are like a tennis game: "Just like the ball goes back and forth across the net in a tennis game, the talking goes back and forth between people in a conversation." Ask the child, "In a tennis game, if one person holds on to the ball the whole time, how does the other person feel?" The child will respond with answers such as "bored" or "left out." Explain that the same is true in a conversation: "The talking needs to go back and forth between people so that one person doesn't feel left out or bored. After talking for a minute, we need to pass the ball to keep the other person involved in the conversation."

You can practice this strategy by passing an actual ball back and forth, explaining that the person holding the ball is the speaker. This activity conveys the reciprocal nature of a conversation in a visual and tactile way. Practice talking for a short time, then pass the ball for someone else to have a turn talking. Note that the "everybody wants to have fun" rule, explained in chapter 7, is also relevant to conversations. All people want to enjoy conversations by being involved and feeling included.

ASK QUESTIONS

Questions promote reciprocity in conversations, and we can teach children on the autism spectrum how to ask questions and listen to the answers. We can help with this skill by working with the child to create a list of questions likely to appeal to a listener's interests, an exercise that also clearly involves social thinking.

One technique that teaches the art of asking questions is called "question of the day." A child reaches into a basket full of three-by-five cards, each of which has one question written on it. The child picks one card, and it is read aloud. The child then chooses two peers or family members to answer the question. This game helps children with initiating or maintaining future conversations because it gives them a repertoire of questions that they can potentially ask any person. It also reinforces whole body listening as the child practices listening to the answers given.

ROLE PLAYING

Role playing is another effective way to teach conversational skills, especially when it comes to asking questions and initiating social interaction. We can identify a relevant situation and assign the child a specific role. Ask him to act out what he would do. For example, a teacher might say "Your classmate Mia just came back from Florida. Before we go talk with her, let's pretend I'm Mia. What could you ask me about the trip?"

We can also set up role-playing situations that give children the opportunity to practice initiating a conversation or asking to join a game. Acting out scenarios allows children to greet others with statements and questions like "Hi, what's your name? What are you playing? Can I play with you guys?"

SCRIPTS

"I just don't know what to say" is a common statement made by autistic children. When children are anxious in a social situation, their anxiety inhibits their ability to determine what they should say or how they should act. One solution to this problem is to provide the child with a predetermined script. Note that this technique is not to be confused with "scripting," which refers to autistic children repeating phrases from books, movies, or television shows. Rather, this strategy refers to helping a child know what to say by giving him the exact language in advance of a situation. Adults can simply tell a child the words he should use or provide a written or visual cue. When taking the second approach, parents and teachers can give the child a card featuring either a picture that signals what he should say or the written words themselves.

These techniques allow children to develop a script in their mind that they can access during times when they would otherwise be unsure of how to proceed. For example, greetings can be a challenge for children on the autism spectrum. When meeting someone for the first time or when seeing a relative or friend, autistic children may launch straight into their favorite topic without first saying hello. Scripts can help with this issue.

For example, in anticipation of a visit to his grandmother's house, tell the child that when he first sees her, he can say, "Hi, Grandma. How are you?" Preview specific scenarios with the child and have him practice his greetings. Promote social thinking by asking him, "What do you think Grandma will think when you greet her so nicely?"

Scripts are also a useful tool for encouraging interaction with peers. Give the autistic child a script of what to say when she sees other children she's interested in joining. For example, tell her, "When you see a group of kids playing and you want to join them, say 'Can I play with you?'" These scripts, as simple as they are, prove to be effective in helping autistic children develop a repertoire of things to say in different social situations.

It's important to help autistic children grasp the basic elements of a successful conversation because conversations are a central part of our daily interactions as human beings. Not only do we regularly communicate important information through even the briefest of verbal exchanges, but we solve problems, plan actions, and build relationships by talking and listening to one another. As this chapter shows, we can help children master the give-and-take that is intrinsic to conversation if we use a range of key strategies. For example, we can play charades to emphasize whole body listening. We can demonstrate the concept of reciprocity by linking an actual dialogue to a game of tennis or catch. And we can also teach the art of asking questions through activities such as role playing.

Understandably, children may sometimes feel intimidated by the sense of possibility and uncertainty that comes with any conversation. After all, we can never be sure of what other people are going to say or how they might respond to our attempts at communicating with them. In this event, we can ease a child's anxiety by emphasizing the conventional nature of many conversations, especially when it comes to initiating a dialogue. We can also provide the child with actual scripts that he can use in commonly occurring situations, such as seeking to join other kids in play.

We want to encourage children to have conversations and support them in their efforts to talk with others. With every successful exchange, they gain self-confidence and build stronger relationships with the people in their lives. The strategies presented in the next chapter will also strengthen a child's confidence and help him see opportunities for social interaction as positive and gratifying experiences.

9

BUILDING SOCIAL CONFIDENCE
ACROSS SETTINGS

Helping children on the autism spectrum feel competent in social situations is the main priority of social skills development. As the previous chapters have shown, it is important to focus on specific areas of social development such as social thinking and conversational skills. However, we cannot forget that anxiety plays a significant role in the social challenges of children with autism. Their fear of the unknown, their worries about being rejected, and their awareness of their own differences are all feelings that can undermine their social engagement and potential for growth.

In addition to teaching children targeted social skills, this chapter shows how to foster feelings of competence and confidence in autistic children—feelings that increase their willingness to enter new social situations and engage with others. By implementing the following techniques and by consciously shaping our own interactions with autistic children, we can help them approach social interactions with a sense of their own capability and self-worth.

MORE PREVIEWING: PREPARE
FOR UNFAMILIAR SITUATIONS

As an offshoot of the general strategy of previewing, we can prepare children for unfamiliar social situations by talking to the child ahead of time about what to expect. We can reduce a child's anxiety and fear of the unknown by giving him the details of an upcoming event. We can give him specifics about what's going to happen, who's going to be there, and how long the event will last.

For example, Emma's family is going to her cousin's christening in the afternoon, but Emma has never been to a christening before and she has no idea what to expect. This uncertainty makes her feel more anxious than usual, and that morning Emma declares that she will not go with her family to the gathering. Emma's mother does not meet her daughter's recalcitrance by forcefully declaring that she must come along with them. Instead she explains the event to Emma so that it won't feel so foreign to her. She describes what a christening is, and she explains what will happen at the ceremony, where it will take place, and who will be there.

Once Emma learns this information about the christening, she goes off by herself to think about the event and ultimately agrees to go. In preparing a child for an unfamiliar situation, we increase predictability and give her some idea of what to expect. This strategy lends structure to an unknown experience, enabling children to plan for an event and to formulate potential questions about what they should do in specific circumstances. This preparation also increases self-regulation because when children know what to expect, they feel more calm and in control of their behavior.

PRACTICE

Practice naturally follows preparing for an unfamiliar event. Once a child is aware of what to expect in a social situation, she can practice her plan and rehearse for a specific event. This helps children feel more secure when they encounter a new social situation because it gives them a sense of mastery over something that is potentially chaotic and unknown.

If we return to our earlier example, we can see how practicing sets Emma up for success at her cousin's christening. Although Emma has agreed to go to the family gathering, she still feels some anxiety about the event because she is unsure how to behave around a baby and how to interact with him. This time her mother responds to Emma's worry with the strategy of practicing. She gets a baby doll, and they rehearse what to say. They first practice asking permission to touch the baby—perhaps his tiny foot—and they prepare for the possibility that Emma's aunt might tell her that she can't touch the baby because she doesn't want him to get germs. If this happens, they practice plan B, which involves playing peekaboo with the baby. They also practice some greetings that Emma can say to her relatives who will be there.

After using this strategy, Emma is much more equipped to deal with an unfamiliar situation because she has a clear plan. She even begins to look forward to the christening. Practice is valuable because it allows children to engage in behavior that they will use in the future. In this way, it instills knowledge, decreases anxiety, and promotes self-regulation.

SPECIFIC REINFORCEMENT

Reinforcement is important in helping autistic children identify and develop positive social skills across different contexts. When children receive attention for positive interactions, they are more likely to understand that these are the skills that are expected and desired and are more likely to try using them again. We want to pinpoint specific social skills for autistic children to practice, and we want to build their self-esteem by praising them for demonstrating the desired behaviors. By offering positive feedback in a specific manner, we can help them identify a consistent set of behaviors to engage in across different social situations.

For example, a teacher might say, "Jade, I like how you shared your clay with Mason; he looks really happy about your choice to give him some clay, too." Not only is this instance of praise clear and specific, but it also models social thinking by indicating what Mason is likely feeling about Jade's actions. Offering specific reinforcement is much more effective than quickly exclaiming something like "Good job!" The specificity of a compliment reinforces a particular social skill while also emphasizing how one's actions influence other people's emotions.

> The specificity of a compliment reinforces a particular social skill while also emphasizing how one's actions influence other people's emotions.

Later in the day, when the teacher sees Jade giving a different classmate a turn on the swing, she can again praise Jade for this specific action. This recognition makes Jade feel confident about her social abilities. It also helps her see that sharing is good in different circumstances.

BUDDY SYSTEM

Having a designated buddy can be useful in helping an autistic child navigate a complex social environment without feeling overwhelmed or singled out for his differences. Ideally, a buddy is a child who is more mature and flexible than his peers and who likes being helpful in an understated way that does not emphasize other people's limitations. A parent or teacher asks the buddy to be a special friend to an autistic child by talking to him, play-ing with him, and generally helping him when he needs it.

A buddy can consistently be a single person or rotate among different peers. A simple explanation to a potential buddy usually works. For example, a teacher might tell her student Emily, "I think you'd have fun playing with Abby today, and you'd be great at helping her make other friends, too. Would you be willing to talk and play with her? Take notice when it seems like she needs help and is unsure of what to do or say." The teacher can take Emily over to Abby, explaining to her that "Emily wants to be your buddy for the day and spend time with you so that you can have fun doing things together and help each other out." When we match children up thought-fully, both kids often find that it's rewarding to have each other as buddies.

MAKING A CONNECTION

Perhaps the most important and yet easily overlooked resource for helping a child grow socially and emotionally is to establish a personal bond with him. Autistic children, as we have seen, might appear to be aloof or stuck in their own worlds at times, but it is imperative for the adults in their lives to reach out to such children and find a way into their world to make a connec-tion with them. The goal of social skills development is ultimately to help children engage with others in a consciously flexible and reciprocal way. It's crucial for adults to model this approach in their interactions with children.

We need to show that we care about a child first and foremost. She must not feel judged, underestimated, or dismissed because her modes of communication and ways of being in the world are different from those of neurotypical people. For all of their social skills challenges, children on the autism spectrum are highly perceptive and often recognize that they don't live up to the expectations of teachers and parents. Because they are likely to feel sad and anxious about this situation, our first step as parents and teachers is to show these children that they matter and that we want to be around them.

In seeking to establish a bond with an autistic child, we need to be flexible ourselves and adjust our own expectations about the rules of suc-cessful social interaction. We need to talk with the autistic children in our lives. We should take the time to sit through a long monologue on occa-sion, showing interest and breaking in periodically to ask a question or express enthusiasm about something the child has said. Although it might seem like we're encouraging poor social skills by enabling the child to persist in his preferred mode of communication, the opposite is true. We are giving the child a reason to want to interact with other people in the first place. We are also helping the child by modeling the skills of engagement and patient listening.

In this way, we live out the social lesson that it can be fun to take part in conversations that don't necessarily proceed as we might choose or expect. The child can see firsthand that someone enjoys hearing about new things and learning about unfamiliar topics. By joining the child in his preferred modes of communication, we lay the foundation for future interactions (Kaufman 2014). On subsequent occasions, the child will seek out engagement and will want to talk with us. Because he feels a sense of trust, he will be more inclined to try out the social strategies that we introduce to him, strategies that will take him out of his comfort zone.

By taking the child's interests and concerns seriously, we also gain vital information that can help him progress. The journalist Ron Suskind describes how tuning in to his autistic son's love of Disney movies was the key to promoting his social development. After family members, teachers, and therapists began speaking to his son Owen by quoting pieces of movie dialogue, Owen began to speak himself and went on to make social and emotional progress that no one initially thought was possible.

After his son went off to college, Suskind reflected on his family's experiences, emphasizing the importance of connecting with autistic children on their own terms: "There's a reason—a good-enough reason—why each autistic person has embraced a particular interest. Find that reason, and you will find them. . . . Authentic interest will help them feel dignity and impel them to show you more, complete with maps and navigational tools that may help to guide their development, their growth" (2014, 339–40).

Don't value an autistic child any less than you would a neurotypical child, even if—especially if—establishing a bond with him feels challenging. Show the child that his thoughts and interests—however intense or eccentric they may be—matter as much to you as the thoughts and interests of his neurotypical peers.

THE TAKEAWAY

When we see autistic children struggling to make friends, play with peers, or engage in conversation, it's important to recognize that these challenges have a neurological basis, stemming from impaired neural connections in the brain. On the whole, autistic children aren't intentionally rude or disinterested in making friends. Rather, their neurodifferences affect theory of mind, making it difficult for them to recognize that other people have thoughts and intentions that don't necessarily coincide with their own.

Although autistic children are quick to absorb the feelings of other people, and though they experience genuine concern for others, they struggle to read facial expressions, body language, and other social cues. In this way, autistic children often miss the signals that convey important information about other people's thoughts and perspectives. Because social interaction can feel inherently chaotic and confusing, autistic children often experience increased anxiety at the prospect of engaging with other people. As a result, they may feel heightened levels of dysregulation, acting out with challenging behavior or retreating into themselves.

Fortunately, through careful guidance and teaching, we can strengthen a child's social skills and alleviate the feelings of anxiety and uncertainty that may overwhelm him on a daily basis. We have outlined strategies that target the specific areas of social thinking and conversational skills to help children recognize other people's interests and give them tools for successfully navigating their interactions with others. We also again recommend the key techniques of previewing and offering reinforcement. When we prepare in advance for unfamiliar social events and reward positive social exchanges across different settings, we make easy interventions that have a major impact on a child's social abilities and experiences.

Finally, we cannot overstate the importance of taking the time to establish a positive rapport with the autistic children in our lives. We need to find out about their passions, pay attention to what they have to say, and use their own interests to promote their social and emotional growth. As we work with autistic children, we also must model the flexibility and perspective taking that we seek to instill in them.

Strategies for Building Social Skills		
Social Thinking	*Conversation Skills*	*Social Confidence*
• Discuss rules for interacting with others • Employ the "look, listen, clarify" technique • Implement social stories • Use the social file metaphor • Read literature to emphasize characters' perspectives	• Practice whole body listening • Demonstrate how conversation is like a tennis game • Teach the art of asking questions • Try role-playing games • Make use of scripts	• Preview new situations • Practice for upcoming events • Reinforce prosocial behavior across settings • Use the buddy system • Make a personal connection with autistic children

Notice how a child responds to the different social strategies you try out, and emphasize the ones that are successful, perhaps returning to other strategies at a later stage. It is also important to be sensitive to social situations that may provoke anxiety. When you see signs that a child is becoming frustrated, anxious, or fearful, offer him opportunities to have downtime, take

As we work with autistic children, we also must model the flexibility and perspective taking that we seek to instill in them.

space, or be alone. Remember that overcoming social challenges is a gradual process that needs to be sustainable for everyone involved. This work is well worth the effort, however, because helping children build social skills establishes a foundation for future growth, enabling them to have successful relationships for the rest of their lives.

IV

ENCOURAGING IMAGINATIVE PLAY

Play is key for a child's cognitive and emotional development. As an activity that promotes communication, social interaction, and other foundational skills, play is an essential ingredient in a child's daily routine. Play is also ubiquitous. Whether kids are outside or inside, whether they are playing a structured game or using their imagination, children love to play. They find that playing is fun, engaging, and intrinsically motivating.

> **Play is a fundamental skill that children use to understand the world.**

Yet not all children share these feelings when it comes to play. For children on the autism spectrum, play can be a trigger for anxiety and dysregulation. The openness and freedom of unstructured play—something that neurotypical children usually delight in—can feel like a sea of overwhelming unpredictability for autistic children, who may struggle to read social cues, think imaginatively, and follow the unspoken rules of spontaneous games. In more structured forms of play involving athletic activities or board games, children on the spectrum may also feel anxious. Having to perform under time pressure, make coordinated movements, manage an atmosphere of excitement, and deal with the prospect of losing are factors that can create significant stress. Activities that many assume are "fun" may cause emotional upheaval for children on the autism spectrum. During recess, free play, or other times of recreation, signs of their distress may become evident in conflicts with peers, withdrawal from social interaction, or episodes of anger or sadness.

ESSENTIALS OF PLAY

Helping autistic children learn to play is essential to promoting self-regulation and overall development. Much more than a form of amusement, play is a complex developmental activity that involves a variety of cognitive, emotional, and social skills. Play aids in children's intellectual development by increasing their problem-solving skills and their capacity for both logical and abstract thinking. In the arena of pretend play, children must be able to think flexibly and creatively, use their imaginations, and explore a variety of social roles. In this sense, imaginative play requires theory of mind, a term that the previous section discusses in depth. As a child inhabits a character or make-believe persona, for example, he must be able to recognize and understand the perspective of another person. This type of pretend play also builds a foundation for future social success by giving children imaginative opportunities to play different roles in cooperation with their peers.

Playing with others helps children grow socially since it requires that they interact and communicate in dynamic ways. It involves engaging in a joint enterprise with others and coordinating activities so that everyone has fun. To this end, play necessitates compromise, sharing, and taking turns. It requires a child not only to communicate her needs and wants, but also to accommodate the needs and wants of her peers. In terms of emotional growth, play is equally valuable because it teaches children coping skills, enhances their ability to identify and express feelings, and increases self-esteem (Greenspan & Wieder, 1998). Play is also a crucial part of building friendships, which are important for many reasons, such as promoting empathy, providing companionship, and decreasing stress (Koegel & Koegel, 1995).

The cognitive, social, and emotional skills that are necessary for play are skills that in turn promote the ability to self-regulate. But these skills, which tend to develop naturally in neurotypical children, do not come so effortlessly to children on the autism spectrum. It's fortunate, then, that play skills can be taught. With the right guidance, we can help children learn to play, offering support as they interact with their peers and engage their capacity for imaginative thinking. It's essential that we encourage autistic children to develop play skills. When we teach children how to play, we teach them how to navigate their world. We provide them with a road map for developing relationships and finding friendships. We help them lay a foundation for healthy interactions with others.

In the chapters that follow, we describe the play skills deficits often seen in autistic children, we explain why these children struggle in play, and we offer strategies that can be used at school and at home to help children find pleasure in using their imaginations and playing cooperatively with others.

10

WHEN PLAYTIME
ISN'T ALL THAT FUN

Whereas neurotypical children generally learn to play spontaneously through their interactions with peers and adults, autistic children often lack the social understanding needed for play because they struggle with joint attention (shared attention with another), reciprocity, and flexibility. Moreover, autistic children frequently have difficulty initiating and sustaining play, and they may also lack the social motivation needed for the development of play skills.

Due to their discomfort and difficulty with social interactions, autistic children often isolate themselves, choosing to play alone. Sometimes they feel more comfortable being off on their own; at other times, though, they desperately want to be with their peers but do not know how to engage with others. Playing alone allows them to avoid the anxiety associated with social interactions. By withdrawing socially, autistic children might find some level of comfort, but they also miss out on the skills and emotional benefits that come from playing with one's peers.

Before we go on to describe techniques for helping children learn the essential skills of play, it's first important to understand *why* autistic children struggle in an arena that so many other children navigate with pleasure and ease.

EGOCENTRIC PLAY: "THE PLAY IS ALL ABOUT ME"

Fran likes to build with blocks and then knock them down. This is the only way he plays with blocks, and he takes great joy in knocking down the blocks, listening to the loud crash and watching the blocks scatter. When he plays blocks with other children, he knocks their block structures down, too. Sometimes the other children yell, "Don't knock down my blocks!" But Fran finds this to be so much fun that he thinks the other kids must find it fun, too. So he continues to knock down their blocks despite their protests. Later, Fran does not understand why kids do not want to play blocks with him.

In this example, Fran's play is egocentric, or self-focused. Lacking a fully developed theory of mind, he struggles to recognize that his peers have a different viewpoint from his own. He thinks that everyone else wants to play with blocks in the same way he does, and he assumes that everyone else knows the rules by which he plays. Fran does not consider that there could be a different way to play with blocks, therefore it does not occur to him to try to accommodate others' wishes.

It's important to note that Fran does not knock down the other children's blocks out of spite, hostility, or aggression. He is simply focused on himself and his preferred method of playing. Fran does not yet have the skills to modify the way he plays with blocks in order to accommodate the other children's desired modes of playing.

RESTRICTED RECIPROCITY IN PLAY: "CAN'T I JUST DO WHAT I WANT?"

Four-year-old Jordan and a friend play Candy Land, a board game they both know how to play. Jordan insists on going first. During the game, when her friend takes too long to move his piece, Jordan moves it for him. Jordan also chooses cards for her friend before he gets a chance to pick for himself. When her friend's piece has to move backward, Jordan laughs with glee that he must go back. But when Jordan is supposed to go back, she quickly cheats and moves her piece forward. As she "wins" the game, Jordan taunts, "Ha ha! I win. You lose." Her friend looks sad. The teacher approaches and asks Jordan, "Is this game just for you to have fun or do we want to make sure everyone has fun?" Jordan responds, "Just for me to have fun."

Given their tendency to engage in egocentric play, children with autism also struggle with reciprocity, the back-and-forth exchange that occurs in play and social interactions. Since they don't readily understand others' perspectives, they don't necessarily internalize that their peers want to have fun, too, and that they want to share equally in the experience by having the same number of turns and the same access to play items. Because their perspective can overshadow everything else, many autistic children are primarily concerned that they have fun themselves, often attempting to win at all costs.

In this example, Jordan plays Candy Land in an egocentric way because she is only concerned about enjoying the game herself. Jordan's efforts to take over and control the game undermine the possibility for reciprocal play. She does not yet understand the value of cooperation and of allowing her friend to take his own turn and to share in the fun. Jordan is largely unaware that her behavior is upsetting to her friend, and she can't make the connection that other peers won't want to play with her when she behaves this way.

Attempting to control the situation is a common tactic used by autistic children to manage the anxiety they experience when playing with their peers. This desire to take charge, however, can make them seem bossy to their peers. As is the case with Jordan, an autistic child may tell people what to do, take others' turns, and cheat or change the rules in order to win.

> When autistic children are inflexible during play, it's not because they are stubborn or oppositional. They simply lack the understanding that there is another way to play that's different from their own.

The goal of winning can eclipse all other aspects and objectives of play, including finishing the game, maintaining self-control, and treating others with fairness and kindness. In a similar vein, losing can represent not only a lack of control, but also feelings of vulnerability and inadequacy. It's therefore not uncommon for autistic children to experience intense frustration and anger upon losing a game—reactions that only exacerbate a child's alienation from peers.

DELAYED DEVELOPMENT OF PRETEND PLAY

Annie loves to play with her dollhouse at home, and she has a certain way that she plays with it. First, she likes to arrange all the furniture on the floor. Second, she chooses each furniture piece carefully and puts it in the correct room. Then she lines up all the dolls on the floor and proceeds to arrange each in a specific spot in the dollhouse. She does not engage in any pretend play with the dollhouse.

When she plays with the dollhouse at school, she repeats this same routine. When other children join her, she insists that they follow her routine, too. The other children play in their own ways, having imaginary conversations and interactions with dolls. But Annie quickly becomes frustrated, insisting that they play the "right" way. When this happens, the other children sometimes get upset and leave. At other times, Annie walks away crying.

In this scenario, Annie is similar to the children in the previous examples because she too struggles with theory of mind and reciprocity. Assuming that her peers want to play with the dollhouse in the exact same manner as she does, Annie does not understand why the other children do not conform to the "correct" way to play. She wants to know why they are doing it "wrong." Annie's routine with the dollhouse is also important because it demonstrates delayed development of pretend play, a common trait among autistic children.

When children have trouble understanding the social world, their capacity for imaginative play is also affected because children develop pretend play skills by observing and imitating others. In struggling to relate to others and imitate their behavior, they do not readily see how various people in their lives can serve as models of how to play. As a result, they miss out on social information that children adapt in playing with dolls, characters, and other make-believe figures.

These social limitations also help to explain why autistic children often do not play with toys in a functional way, preferring instead to engage in repetitive routines by lining up play items, for example, or organizing them in other ways. Although neurotypical people might think that this type of play does not look like fun, it appeals to some autistic children because it's predictable, orderly, and structured. This form of play brings control and a sense of calm to a world that frequently seems confusing. When other children attempt to change their orderly play routine, autistic children may become annoyed or frustrated.

In addition to being unpredictable, pretend play involves abstract thinking, a mode of cognition that can prove challenging for some autistic children. We think abstractly while pretending; abstract thinking is what enables us to imagine things that are not there, invent scenarios, and project the potential consequences of specific actions. In pretend play, children also use symbols to represent people, objects, and ideas. But because autistic children often think concretely, they struggle to understand the point of pretend play. In their minds, for example, a stuffed animal is simply a stuffed animal. How can it go on a picnic and have a tea party?

USE OF SCRIPTS IN PLAY

Andrew and Eli decide to play superhero figures together, using Batman's toy Batcave as the setting for their play. Although Andrew desperately wants Eli to play with him, he grows increasingly frustrated because Eli is not moving and placing the figures in the "right" way. The play goes smoothly for a couple of minutes, but it's then interrupted by Andrew complaining in a loud voice, "No, Eli, Batman is supposed to go inside the Batcave, not up on the roof!" Eli says he's sorry and moves Batman as instructed, but moments later there is another outburst from Andrew, who exclaims, "No, no, no! The Batmobile doesn't fly like that. And it's not time for Batman to be in the Batmobile yet. First, he has to get the Joker, and that needs to happen here outside the Batcave. Don't you know anything?"

What Eli does not, in fact, know is that Andrew is trying to re-create a story from a Batman comic book he recently received. In this case he is relying on a script, another form of play that appeals to autistic children because it's orderly and predictable.

Because autistic children often have underdeveloped resources for play involving acts of fantasy and imagination, they might turn to scripting (Coplan, 2010). While it may look like they are playing with things like dolls or *Star Wars* figures in a spontaneous way, there is a chance that autistic children are using the toys at hand to re-create a narrative that they have encountered in a book or seen in a film or television show.

There is comfort in sameness.

In this type of scripted play, it's obviously difficult for peers to be equal participants, for they may not understand that their autistic friend is following an unspoken story line and feels compelled to re-create it with precision. This situation can be frustrating for both children. While the neurotypical child may grow tired of being "bossed around," the autistic child likely feels that it's natural to re-create a scene from a comic book or movie, and he thinks that others should share in following the script even if they do not know that this is the plan.

DIFFICULTY MAINTAINING PLAY

Caroline begins playing with a group of peers in the play kitchen at preschool, but she does not understand what she should say or do as her classmates pretend to cook a surprise birthday dinner for the teacher. After three minutes, she moves to the block area and starts building a tower of blocks. In the process, she takes a block from another peer who yells at her. Abandoning her tower after two minutes, she goes to the dress-up area and begins trying on hats. She grabs a hat from a peer and puts it on her head. When the peer demands the hat back, Caroline gives it to her and heads to the train table. When she can't immediately access the train car she wants, Caroline's frustration reaches a tipping point, and she pushes a peer out of the way, knocking him to the floor, so that she can grab the train.

Caroline's experience offers a glimpse into a scene that is all too common when an autistic child attempts to negotiate playtime in school. Children on the autism spectrum frequently have difficulty maintaining engagement in play. Like Caroline, they may move quickly from one play item or play space to another. This lack of consistent engagement may be due to impulsivity or a short attention span, both of which make children easily distracted by other activities or stimuli in the environment. Additionally, because of the social challenges that autistic children experience, as described in part III, they especially can struggle with initiating interactions and maintaining play.

One way that children cope with these stressors is by limiting and abruptly ending social interactions. When a child starts to feel anxious or frustrated while playing, she simply moves on to a different activity in an effort to reduce her worry, irritation, and potential anger. The anxiety she experiences accumulates with each stressful interaction, and by the time she has made her third or fourth attempt at playing, she may feel exasperated. The people around her may not be aware of the child's growing distress, and when she becomes upset, there appears to be no obvious reason for her emotional outburst.

But from the child's perspective, anxiety and frustration have been building to the point that she can't contain these feelings any longer. In these instances, some adults report that the child "just got angry out of nowhere." But, as in Caroline's case, there is an underlying cause for the challenging behavior. The adults are simply unaware that the child's anger has been building across a series of unsuccessful social interactions.

RIGIDITY IN PLAY

George, age five, plays bingo for the first time with a group of four peers. Though he listens while the teacher explains the rules, he misunderstands how the game works and thinks that he will get a match on every turn and quickly win the game. However, as he begins to play, he realizes that the game does not meet his expectations at all. In his mind, there is one way that the game is played, and he becomes disappointed, frustrated, and angry when it does not turn out as he expects.

Even though the teacher repeats the directions to him, explaining that no one gets a match on every turn, George can't resume the game with a fresh understanding of the rules. He already has it set in his mind that he should get a match on each turn, and because this has not happened, he dismisses the whole game as "stupid." He exclaims that he never wants to play bingo again. From George's perspective, bingo is dumb because it's frustrating and unpredictable; you never know when you might get a match. The next time the group plays bingo, George refuses to join in and declares that the game "stinks."

In this example, George's thinking is so rigid that it prevents him from joining his peers in a form of group play. He expects the game to proceed as he thinks it should. Once he learns the correct way to play, it's too late for him to adjust his expectations. He lacks the spontaneity needed to adjust to what he perceives as an entirely new set of rules. He even wonders if the rules might change on him again.

When the game does not meet his narrow idea of the way things should go, he becomes upset and disinterested in playing. George's rigidity is also exacerbated by the fact that bingo has a definitive yet unpredictable outcome—there is a clear way to win, but no one ever knows if he will get a match. Winning is just a matter of luck. This unpredictability provokes a great deal of anxiety. Just when a child thinks he is about to win, another player can suddenly call out "bingo," derailing the child's expectations and anticipated accomplishment. At every turn, the game thwarts George's desire to know what to expect and to emerge as the winner.

LIMITED COGNITIVE PROCESSING OF SOCIAL INFORMATION

Four-year-old Daniel plays ball with a group of peers who are kicking the ball back and forth to each other on the playground. Many children are talking and yelling. Daniel kicks the ball several times to children who aren't looking at him and not expecting to receive the ball. After several minutes, Daniel picks up the ball and runs with it, expecting the other children to chase him. The other children become annoyed that Daniel has run away with the ball and yell for him to bring the ball back. Later the children tease him and call him a "ball hog." Daniel does not understand what this means as he imagines a pig in the shape of a ball.

Daniel's struggles with this informal playground game are commonly seen in children on the autism spectrum. He does not understand the unwritten rules of the game, that a player can't simply change a soccer game into a chase game without first talking to the others who are playing.

Daniel also finds it difficult to participate successfully in the soccer game because he can't read the social cues and body language of his peers. He does not know to make eye contact and kick the ball at the children who are looking at him.

All the visual and verbal stimulation makes the game confusing for Daniel. He does not yet have the cognitive processing abilities to interpret the multiple messages of play conveyed at once by the other children's words, nonverbal behavior, and social cues. His concrete thinking is also a mismatch for the fast-paced and frequently changing play that constitutes the soccer game. Not recognizing Daniel's challenges, the other children think that he's trying to ruin their game deliberately. They tease him for messing everything up; their teasing, in turn, deters Daniel from playing again.

MOTOR SKILLS AND COORDINATION CHALLENGES

Phillip really wants to play soccer with the other children on the playground, but he knows he gets off-balance easily and can't aim the ball. Many times, he misses the ball when he tries to kick it. He has been teased in the past when trying to play soccer with peers, so he decides to walk around the playground by himself instead of trying to play soccer. He feels left out, inferior, and sad. He wonders what is wrong with him since he can't play like the other kids his age.

Children on the autism spectrum frequently have delayed development of motor skills and coordination, a topic discussed in more detail in part V of this book. For now, however, it's sufficient to note that many playground activities and sports can be especially challenging for autistic children. When it comes to hopscotch, jump rope, or other games such as soccer, baseball, or basketball, autistic children often struggle to succeed because they do not yet possess the physical skills that these modes of play require. They tend to lack core strength, balance, and eye-hand coordination; they may also have trouble more basically with perceiving how their bodies are positioned in space.

When engaging in athletic activities, children like Phillip frequently feel inferior to their peers because they can't understand why everyone else performs with such agility and speed while they struggle to master basic movements. For this reason, developmental delays in gross motor skills and coordination often exacerbate self-isolative behavior, low self-esteem, and feelings of frustration.

AVOIDANCE OF PLAY WITH PEERS

Michael prefers to play alone in his room. He likes to watch Disney movies, repeat lines from Disney movies, line up Disney figures on his bureau, and play with his Rubik's Cube. When he is at school, he chooses to play by himself, usually lining up cars or dinosaurs. He does not initiate any interaction with peers. When other peers get too close to his play space, he gets up and moves away. He feels most calm and comfortable when he is alone. Interactions with people make him feel anxious and vulnerable, so he avoids them as much as possible.

Like many children with autism, Michael does not find play with his peers intrinsically motivating. With underdeveloped social and play skills, autistic children often see play with peers as something that is inherently confusing and anxiety provoking. It's a natural and self-protective tendency for Michael to avoid upsetting situations. Removing himself from the possibility of peer interaction reinforces his preference to be alone. Even though many autistic children often spend time on their own, they desperately may want to play with others but are dissuaded by the feelings of vulnerability that they experience after their prior attempts at play prove to be unsuccessful. They may express the desire to play like neurotypical kids and wish they had the skills to do so.

It is all too often the case that we find autistic children like Michael playing by themselves. Given their challenges with social skills and theory of mind, playtime isn't always fun for children on the spectrum. As we have seen, their play tends to be egocentric and lacking in reciprocity, and their interests often eclipse the perspectives of their peers. More specifically, autistic children may have difficulty seeing beyond both their own desire to win and their own methods for playing with certain toys. Children with autism also are often concrete thinkers who like sameness and predictability. These traits make it hard for them to engage in pretend play and to enact made-up scenarios that don't follow a predetermined script or pattern.

When it comes to playing games with a group, autistic children often struggle to think flexibly and manage unpredictable outcomes that involve winning or losing. They also may have difficulty with athletic games, as these require players to process social information from multiple sources and to make fast and coordinated movements. Given the different challenges autistic children face when it comes to play, it's not surprising that they abruptly may limit their play interactions or resort to spending time alone. But in the next chapter we explore effective strategies for helping autistic children develop play skills so that they can gain confidence and enjoy spending time with their peers.

11

TEACHING PLAY AND
BUILDING IMAGINATION

It bears repeating that play is essential to the education and development of all children, including those who are on the autism spectrum. Play serves as a foundation from which to build relationships and understand the world. Through play, children develop social skills and discover how to make friends. Play also helps children gain skills of self-regulation in the long term because it strengthens their ability to communicate, solve problems, and cope with strong emotions. If children do not know how to play alongside their peers, they may appear lost in a sea of activity. Their development hinges on learning to play.

A small group of both neurotypical and autistic children is usually the ideal setting for teaching play skills. It's mutually beneficial for autistic children to play with their neurotypical peers. Neurotypical children can model play skills for autistic children and challenge them to learn to take turns, use their imaginations, and be cooperative and friendly. Autistic children can help neurotypical children become more flexible and inclusive by involving them in new types of play and showing them that not all people experience the world in the same way. It can also be effective to teach autistic children play skills in other situations, such as in a group comprised of other children on the spectrum or in one-on-one interactions with a parent or teacher.

This chapter offers some key strategies that can be used at home or school for teaching autistic children how to play. Whether you have an hour or only a few minutes, these practical, evidence-based strategies are effective in helping children learn to play and develop their imaginations.

FOLLOW THE CHILD'S LEAD

Jonathan, a four-year-old autistic boy, plays by himself in a play area at preschool while two other boys build a ramp nearby. Jonathan carefully puts toy vehicles into a toy garage.

His teacher, Mrs. Smith, sits on the floor next to Jonathan and watches for a moment. "Those are some cool cars," she says enthusiastically. Jonathan says nothing in reply. "I really like the red sports car. I've always wanted one of those," she says. "My favorite one is the green tow truck," Jonathan says. "It reminds me of Mater from the Cars *movie," says Mrs. Smith. She then picks up another car and asks, "Do you think we could fit this one in the garage, too?" "Sure," responds Jonathan, who takes the car and puts it in the garage alongside the other cars.*

**Join the child in what he is doing.
Meet the child where he is.**

In this scene, Mrs. Smith joins Jonathan on the floor, getting down to his level. This is a simple but important first step in working with an autistic child who can feel easily intimidated by adults standing over him, leaning over him, or looking down on him. The idea is to move your body to physically match the child's position. If he is sitting at a table, sit at the table with him. If he is sitting on the floor, sit on the floor with him. If he is standing on the jungle gym, stand with him on the jungle gym. Your effort to share the same physical space as the child shows your willingness to join the child, to relate to him, and to develop a rapport. Being on the same level physically is the foundation from which to further establish a relationship with the child.

Mrs. Smith is also quiet and calm while she initially watches Jonathan. She then makes several comments to show her interest in the cars. By simply showing interest in what he is doing, Mrs. Smith finds common ground with Jonathan and builds a base upon which she can interact with him further to help promote play skills. In this way she meets the child where he is, at his developmental and skill level. She engages him and seeks reciprocal communication, gently urging him into actions that are fundamental to the play process. Mrs. Smith then joins Jonathan in what he is doing; she follows his lead in putting vehicles in the garage. This sensitivity to Jonathan's interests helps him feel secure with Mrs. Smith as a playmate.

EXPAND ON THE PLAY

The next day, Jonathan is again playing with the cars in the toy garage, lining up the cars on the carpet. He finds comfort in the structure and predictability in doing the same thing. Mrs. Smith joins him on the carpet again. This time, she takes the red sports car and runs it along the carpet, saying, "Zoom, zoom, here comes my favorite car!" She parks it alongside Jonathan's cars. Using a high-pitched voice to pretend the car is talking, she says, "Is it okay if I park here, Mister?" Jonathan looks at her quizzically, then smiles and responds, "Sure." "I really like the headlights on your car, Mister," she comments in the same high-pitched tone. "Thanks," says Jonathan. Mrs. Smith continues speaking for the car, "I'm going to that ramp over there. Do you want to come?"

As she finishes her sentence, she runs her car along the carpet to a car ramp and pushes it down the ramp, saying excitedly, "Hurray!" Jonathan giggles. "Yippee! This is fun. I want to do this again," she exclaims in her high-pitched voice for the car. She pushes her car down the ramp several more times. Later in the day, Mrs. Smith observes Jonathan using the ramp with his car, and he seems amused.

Here, Mrs. Smith builds on the relationship she has established with Jonathan. She uses the original play scheme that Jonathan developed—lining up cars—and she expands it into a new play scenario so that the cars move along the carpet, slide down a ramp, and talk to one another. It's important that she introduces this new play scheme with excitement, showing how much fun it is to play with cars in this different way. Her enthusiastic and warm demeanor promotes interaction and reduces the potential for resistance and avoidance on the part of the child.

Mrs. Smith shows Jonathan that it's not only fun to play with cars, but also fun to play with other people. Having fun while engaging in play with others is an important concept for children on the autism spectrum, who, as we have seen, often like to play alone. Showing them the fun and excitement of playing with others is essential to introducing interactive play. Mrs. Smith accomplishes this goal by allowing Jonathan to retain a sense of control. She does not completely take over the play scheme nor does she make any demands on Jonathan. She simply introduces a new play scenario, acts it out, and asks if Jonathan wants to join in. Using an animated voice to keep Jonathan's interest, she essentially becomes part of the play.

TEACH PRETEND PLAY

Mrs. Smith also introduces the concept of pretend play in this scenario. She creatively undermines Jonathan's tendency to play in repetitive and rigid ways by offering imaginative possibilities for the cars he likes to line up. She shows him that they can come alive, that they can say funny and interesting things, and that they can become part of a story. In this way, a toy car is transformed from an item that can be lined up into a play object that represents something else. Making this connection helps Jonathan begin to develop symbolic play, which entails using one object to represent something else, like pretending a ribbon is a butterfly.

It's important that Mrs. Smith expands Jonathan's repertoire of play simply by modeling how to pretend. Demonstrating how she uses her imagination is a powerful tool, for children will begin to mimic the pretend play modeled for them and then develop their own pretend play schemes. For example, after seeing that the cars can take on imaginary roles, Jonathan learns that he can make other objects pretend to talk, like a stuffed bear and a helicopter. He begins to create conversations with different toys and play objects. Here we see that Mrs. Smith has successfully helped Jonathan establish a "toolbox" of pretend play skills that he can use in any situation when an opportunity for imaginative play arises.

Techniques for Teaching Pretend Play

There are many ways to help children develop pretend play skills. The key is to find your inner child and act like a kid! Show excitement, demonstrate imaginative ideas, crawl around on the floor, and have fun. Ultimately, our goal is to teach children to play with other children, so acting like a child helps to prepare autistic children for playing with others. Showing excitement and enthusiasm also aids in keeping autistic children attentive and engaged. Try not to feel embarrassed. The more you model pretend play, the better you will get at it and the more fun you will have. Other kids will think it is fun, too. There are opportunities to pretend everywhere, as the following suggestions demonstrate.

- Take on the role of another character. Pretend you are a bug, an airplane, a superhero, or a monster. Pretend you are flying, eating, driving.
- Turn one object into another object. A chair becomes a mountain. A couch becomes a slide. A box becomes a garage.
- Play dress up and act like an elderly grandmother or play the role of a doctor or mechanic.
- Make characters (dolls, play animals, vehicles) go to a dance party, a tea party, or a picnic. Take them on a trip to the zoo or a journey to outer space. Regularly introduce new ideas about what different characters can do and where they can pretend to go.

USE PRETEND PLAY TO BUILD SKILLS

We can create imaginative scenarios that help children develop important skill sets at the same time that they learn the essentials of play. By directing the play to target specific aspects of social, cognitive, and emotional development, we can help children develop strength in these areas while also having fun with them and making play a rewarding experience.

Problem Solving

Create problems for the child to solve during pretend play. For example, if a toy car gets stuck on the edge of the carpet, pretend that it's stuck in the mud. Exclaim, "Oh no! The car is stuck in the mud. What should we do?" Ask the child additional questions to help solve the problem: "What are we going to do to get the car out? Is that a tow truck over there? Do you think he could help us?" *Do not solve the problem for the child.* Ask questions to guide him to the answer. Some children will need just one question; others will need many more.

Expression of Feelings

Pretend play can help children learn about their emotions, enhancing their ability to express their feelings, label different bodily sensations, and identify the causes of particular emotions. Pretend play is a wonderful, nonthreatening way to teach emotions in a manner that children find fun and authentic. The suggestions that follow offer concrete ways of adapting pretend play to strengthen a child's emotional intelligence.

- *Describe the emotional content of the play using specific terms.* Attribute feelings to the characters in a play scheme and label these explicitly, making sure to address a range of emotions such as excitement, happiness, sadness, anger, and fear. Verbalize emotions on behalf of the play figures so that children can connect feelings with words and actions. While the dolls are dancing, comment, "They seem very excited!" When the bear is lost, say, "He seems sad and worried that he can't find his way." Also help children connect emotions with bodily sensations and gestures by saying something like, "The Hulk balled up his fists and grunted when he was mad" (Greenspan & Wieder, 1998).

- *Describe the emotional themes of the play scheme as these unfold in the story you create.* Invent scenarios in which characters seek power, show concern, or freeze in fear. Make comments that emphasize the connections among feelings, character traits, and actions. For example, you might say, "That truck is powerful! It's pulling three cars." Or "the train engine is controlling all the other cars."
- *Describe how behavior affects the emotions of others.* This technique ultimately helps children make connections between their actions and how other people feel as a result. For example, you might explain that "The elephant called the lion names, and now the lion is sad" or "The tiger gets mad and roars at the bear when the bear hits him."
- *Introduce new emotions with which the child is unfamiliar.* For example, have a character express vulnerability and create an opportunity for another character to show care and concern by saying, "I am confused. I don't know what to do. I need help." In another scenario you might say, "When the animals couldn't go to the park, they felt disappointed."

SOCIAL INTERACTION

In being a child's active play partner, you have many opportunities to promote social skills by encouraging reciprocal conversation, demonstrating nonverbal communication, and signaling the intentions behind certain actions. Here are some strategies that aim to promote social skills during pretend play.

- *Develop conversations between dolls, superheroes, dinosaurs, or other characters.* Demonstrate how a reciprocal conversation goes back and forth between imaginary figures without one person dominating the conversation. Using dolls, for example, parents and teachers can act out a simple scenario like the following exchange. Barbie says to Ken, "Let's go get ice cream." Ken responds, "I need to find my shoes first." Barbie responds, "I'll help you!" Ken says, "Thanks." As you model reciprocal conversation for the child, slowly increase the dialogue. Encourage children to take on the role of one of the characters and join in the conversation.
- *Develop communication skills, stressing how we can use language to get our needs met.* Have specific characters articulate what they want in a given moment. For example, have Superman say, "I really wanted to

fly to the park, not drive." Emphasize that people understand what Superman wants when he tells us what he is thinking: "Now that Superman has used his words, I understand what he wants."

- *Show how to initiate play.* Invent a scenario that acts out how a character can make a connection with another character to initiate social interaction. For example, in pretend play say, "Wonder Woman really wants to play with Spider-Man but she's not sure what to do." Then using your best Wonder Woman impersonation, say, "Hey Spider-Man, do you want to play?" Then Spider-Man responds, "Sure!"

- *Teach restitution and intention.* It can be hard for children on the autism spectrum to verbalize the intentions and motivations behind their actions. Describing the intentions of the characters during pretend play gives children a language they can eventually adopt themselves. For example, you might explain that "the pink pony made the rainbow pony cry because she refused to eat the chocolate cake that the rainbow pony baked, saying that it was gross." However, you can then explain that "the pink pony didn't mean to hurt rainbow pony's feelings. It's just that she always gets a stomachache when she eats chocolate and that's why she didn't want the cake." This scenario can then be expanded to teach restitution and to resolve the conflict by making the original intention clear. The pink pony can say to the rainbow pony: "I'm sorry. I didn't want the cake because chocolate makes my tummy upset. Can we make a strawberry cake together instead?" In play scenarios like this one, we can ask questions along the way to highlight the importance of knowing the motivation for certain actions and behavior. Ask things like "Where are they going?" or "What are they going to do now?" (Greenspan & Wieder, 1998).

In teaching autistic children how to develop the skills needed for pretend play, it's useful overall to mimic what other children of the same age might do in various scenarios. We want children to gain experience in facing the challenges that they are likely to encounter while playing with their peers. Calling attention to conflicts in the realm of imaginative play prepares children to handle similar situations in real life.

For example, insist on getting your way. If the child wants the plane to crash into the city of blocks you've just built, suggest instead that the plane crash into the ocean and explain that you don't want all of your hard building work to be wiped out in an instant. If a child takes a play item from you, aim to take it back and model the coping and problem-solving skills appropriate for the situation. If Jonathan grabs a toy dinosaur from Mrs. Smith, for example, she can say, "Hey, I'm playing with that dinosaur," just as a peer might say. If Jonathan doesn't give back the dinosaur, then provide him with the social skill that he needs, instructing him, in this case, to ask for the toy instead of taking it.

In addition to learning these lessons, it's important that autistic children come to understand the fundamentals of imaginative play not only because we want them to discover new ways of having fun, but also because play provides valuable opportunities for learning important social and emotional skills. As this chapter shows, we can first work to gain a child's interest in play by establishing a bond with him and engaging him in a nonintimidating way. For example, we should initially follow the child's lead and meet him on his level, both in physical and emotional terms. This means that we should show interest in what the child is doing and join him in that activity. We can slowly stretch the child's play schemes by first making our own contributions to a certain scenario and then by expanding on it and enriching it with symbolic meaning. We can eventually create new play schemes in consultation with the child, and, as these evolve, we can incorporate a variety of techniques designed to engage him in pretend play.

In our interactions with children, we can also consciously shape the imaginative content of play to bolster key skills that are essential for achieving self-regulation. We can direct our play with toys and figures so that these objects come to life as characters who need the child to help them with things like solving problems and managing conflicts. If we use our imaginations to give these characters rich social and emotional lives, then we have limitless opportunities for teaching about feelings and social dynamics in a fun and spontaneous way. For example, we can demonstrate the art of conversation by making dolls or superheroes talk to each other. We can also teach a great deal about emotions by devising imaginative scenarios that highlight important lessons such as the connections between specific actions and feelings. Overall, when we help children learn to engage in pretend play, we also build skills that enable to them to self-regulate in other aspects of life. They learn to compromise, think flexibly, and see things from a different perspective. We continue to target these skills and to promote social development more generally as we turn to the next chapter to explore techniques for encouraging play with peers.

12

FACILITATING PLAY WITH PEERS

It goes without saying that we should include peers in teaching autistic children how to play successfully with others. It's ideal to facilitate peer-based play in a school setting or structured play group composed of neurotypical children, children on the autism spectrum, or a mixture of both groups. In settings that involve neurotypical children, it's first important to consider the possibility of revealing to the group or class that a peer has autism.

If the parents grant permission beforehand, it may be helpful to lead a class discussion about autism to explain that one of the children in the group is autistic. Ask the parents ahead of time if they would like their child to be present for this conversation or if they would like to be present themselves. During group or circle time, the adults can introduce the topic of autism, explaining what it is and describing how autistic children have both special strengths and needs. The class can consider not only how they might help the child with autism, but also how their autistic friend can help them by using any of his special talents to assist in solving problems or completing projects, for example. There are also books for children that explain the basics of autism on their level.

If the parents aren't comfortable with their child being identified as autistic, it's possible to have a more general conversation about autism, especially since it's likely that young children already know—or will eventually encounter—other kids who are on the spectrum. Raising the topic of autism is an excellent way to teach children that some people experience the world differently and that there is value in having a different perspective.

Let us now turn to the specific strategies that promote play with peers. As with the other strategies in this book, these research-proven techniques can be implemented not only at school, but also at home with siblings and friends.

DESIGNATE A PLAY PARTNER

Sara, a neurotypical five-year-old in preschool, agrees to assist with a pretend play game after Mrs. Smith explains that her classmate Jonathan needs a little extra encouragement to play with other people. Seeing that Jonathan is in his favorite play area putting cars on a shelf, Mrs. Smith tells Sara to approach Jonathan and ask him if she can play with the cars, too. Sara does this, and she sits with Jonathan and begins to build a track for the cars. Mrs. Smith then sits with Sara and Jonathan and comments, "Sara is building a track. I wonder what we can do with the track." Sara responds, "We can play with the cars on the track." Mrs. Smith responds, "That's a great idea. Let's play with the cars on the track." Mrs. Smith and Sara play with cars on the track, commenting on how fast they are going, which cars they like, and how much fun it is. Jonathan watches carefully, and after three minutes, he joins in, putting his cars on the track and smiling.

In order to encourage Jonathan to engage in play with a peer, Mrs. Smith first identifies a student who is especially caring and flexible. She then acts as a facilitator, enabling Sara to join in an activity that already amuses Jonathan and makes him feel comfortable. Mrs. Smith explicitly verbalizes her intentions and actions while playing with Sara so that Jonathan can understand the purpose and function of the play. Her words also provide subtle encouragement for Jonathan to join in by emphasizing the structure and predictability of the play. This encouragement also emerges as Mrs. Smith and Sara model how to play. Neither pressures Jonathan to join in, and it's clear that he can choose whether or not to play cars along with them.

In this situation, if Jonathan had not joined in the play spontaneously, Mrs. Smith could have then requested that Sara ask Jonathan if he would like to play with the track. It's often more effective for a peer to ask the autistic child to join in because the peer's invitation to play makes the child with autism feel more confident socially, affirming that other kids like his company and see him as a potential friend. Once the child agrees to play in response to the peer's request, the adult then has a great opportunity to encourage reciprocity, helping the children to share the track, to take turns, and to have fun *together.*

The goals of designating a play partner are to help the autistic child engage with another peer either in parallel play or, preferably, in cooperative play. This strategy also aims to encourage autistic children to take part in reciprocal interactions and new play schemes. Overall, the idea is to help the autistic child come to recognize that playing with peers is just as fun—if not more fun—than playing alone. The hope is that, ultimately, a social relationship develops between the autistic child and the play partner wherein the two children grow and learn together, needing less adult intervention over time.

FACILITATE GROUP PLAY

Mrs. Smith notices Jonathan playing by himself at the sand table, transferring sand from one cup to another. Billy, a neurotypical peer, is not engaged in any play, and Mrs. Smith invites him over to the sand table. As Billy begins moving sand with a toy dump truck, Mrs. Smith comments, "Wow, Billy. That dump truck really moves a lot of sand. I wonder if it could move some sand over to Jonathan. It looks like he needs some more." Billy proceeds to shove sand toward Jonathan's area. Jonathan scoops up the sand with a cup and puts it in a sieve. Mrs. Smith comments, "That's cool how the sand goes through the sieve. I wonder if we could put some in the dump truck." Jonathan then takes it upon himself to move the sieve so that the sand lands in the dump truck. Billy says, "Thanks. Here's another truck to fill up," at which point Jonathan fills another truck with sand. After three minutes, Mrs. Smith leaves the boys to continue playing on their own.

In this example, Mrs. Smith informally and spontaneously invites another peer to go to a play area where Jonathan is engaged in a rather rigid play scheme of moving sand from cup to cup. She does not interact directly with Jonathan at first, but she nonetheless draws him to play in a subtle manner by asking if Billy's dump truck can bring Jonathan some sand. After Jonathan puts the sand from Billy in a sieve, Mrs. Smith shows enthusiasm about Jonathan's actions and suggests a way that the two boys can play together using the sieve to fill up more dump trucks. In this way, she shows Jonathan that you can fill up trucks with sand, introducing him to a new play scheme. And by including a peer, Mrs. Smith also encourages reciprocal interaction between the boys with Billy offering a truck and Jonathan filling it up.

Because Mrs. Smith helps initiate this play scheme in a neutral and unobtrusive manner, she can easily step back to allow the children to continue to play more independently. In her simple, short interaction with the boys, Mrs. Smith helps Jonathan achieve several goals. He has been able to expand on a play scheme, learn a new play scheme, engage with a peer, and practice reciprocal interactions in cooperative play. Jonathan has also had fun while achieving all of these goals. Hopefully, this successful experience increases Jonathan's confidence and motivation to play with others.

VIDEO RECORD PLAY WITH PEERS

Many children on the autism spectrum are visual learners and enjoy watching videos. With the permission of a child's parents, we can make this form of enjoyment a learning tool by using a cell phone or an iPad to record an autistic child playing with his peers. We can then send the video to the parents so that the child can review the play scene whenever he wants outside of school. Choose a play interaction that captures the child successfully executing any number of play skills such as reciprocity, sharing, having fun with others, initiating peer interaction, and communicating intent or feelings. Watching the video recording reinforces these skills and builds self-confidence as the child sees himself enjoying interaction with other children and maintaining engagement with his peers. You can record children playing in a natural setting, or you can set up a specific scene and dialogue with the help of other children. Both are effective in helping children learn to play.

TEACH CHILDREN WHAT TO EXPECT

Jonathan plays a game of musical chairs at preschool. He does not share that it's his first time playing this game, and he quickly feels confused because children are fighting over being able sit in a chair. The excitement of the game overwhelms him, and at one point he shoves another child out of the way to reach a chair, and the child falls down. When the child becomes upset, Jonathan does not understand what he has done wrong because it seems to him that pushing and shoving are part of the game.

Mrs. Smith recognizes Jonathan's confusion, and she sees that he is growing agitated. So she calls a halt to the game and tells the class, "It's important that we all agree to the same rules for the game so that everyone can have fun." She then reviews the rules for musical chairs and prepares the children for the possibility that they will be out of the game when they don't reach a chair in time. She explains that being out is a part of the game, and she gives them a plan for when they are out. She tells the children that they can clap their hands and tap their toes to the beat of the music, which gives them a purpose, helps them stay involved, and keeps them entertained while waiting.

Games like musical chairs are especially challenging for autistic children because they are fundamentally unpredictable. Their excitement derives from not knowing what to expect, but as previously discussed, children on the autism spectrum easily become upset with change and uncertainty. Additionally, the thought of losing a game that no one can control feels like an affront to logic and common sense. Children with autism thrive on having a plan because structure and predictability help them feel safe and more comfortable. Fortunately, as the following list shows, we can incorporate various techniques to help make play more predictable and therefore more enjoyable for autistic children. Not every strategy is applicable to all types of games; choose techniques that are the best fit for a particular activity.

- *Preview.* When teaching a new game, review it ahead of time with the child so that he knows what to expect. Assume the child does *not* know the expectations. In the earlier example, Jonathan can overcome his confusion once Mrs. Smith previews the expectations and rules for musical chairs. He also stays regulated once he is out of the game because he has a plan that gives him something to do instead of waiting on the sidelines and stewing about having lost.
- *Make a list of the rules.* Autistic children, as we have seen, are frequently rule followers. They think concretely, and they understand that rules are to be followed, not broken. Making a list of rules for a game helps them understand expectations so that everyone can be on the same page about how to play. Writing the list assists children in understanding the rules, highlighting the clear and concrete nature of the game.
- *Use visual supports.* Because autistic children are often visual learners, it can be helpful to incorporate a picture schedule describing the steps of a game or coordinated play. A picture schedule is especially beneficial for teaching peer-based play because it separates multiple and potentially confusing activities, prompting a child to make the right move at the right time. It's also useful to make simple comic strips with stick figures to explain the expectations for play. A comic strip about musical chairs, for example, might feature three to five panels showing children walking around chairs, keeping hands to themselves, moving a chair out of the circle, and sitting to the side when they get out. This exercise does not require any artistic ability, and it can be done in a matter of minutes while the child observes.
- *Use a mantra.* Use a phrase repeatedly and have the child repeat it after you to reinforce a certain rule of play. In the example above, the phrase "It's just part of the game" is a useful mantra to normalize the experience of being out once you don't have a chair. As a way of preparing for a potentially difficult outcome, mantras are an important tool for promoting self-regulation when a child may be disappointed or upset.

- *Just watch.* Suggest that the child first watch a game or play interaction and then join in when he feels comfortable. Learning through observation is a powerful tool that helps to lower the child's anxiety about unfamiliar tasks.
- *Give the child control.* There are many opportunities during play for children to give input, make decisions, and make choices. When possible, allow autistic children to feel some control during the play in order to help them feel more comfortable and regulated. For example, the child can pick the music to be played during musical chairs. When playing a game at home, let the child decide where to play, choosing between the living room or kitchen, for example. The child also could choose to play the game before or after a snack.
- *Make sure everyone is having fun.* One easy way to help a child feel in control is to put him in charge of making sure everyone is having fun, as described in chapter 7.
- *Explain that game play sometimes varies.* Because autistic children might not understand that some children play games a little differently from how they do, they may be insistent that the other children play their way, the way "it's supposed to be played." Before anyone starts playing, explain to the children that there is more than one version of the same game and that some children have a version that is different from the autistic child's preferred method. Have children agree on what version they are playing ahead of time.
- *Offer an "out."* Give a child the opportunity to remove himself from the game and take a break if he is feeling upset or frustrated. It's important for children to have a safe place to go in order to promote self-regulation. We do not want a child to feel "stuck" or trapped. Direct him to a cozy spot or "cool down" area that's available to any child who needs it.

MORE PRACTICE: DO A TRIAL RUN

Jonathan really wants to play kickball with some classmates, but he is too afraid to ask to join in and is worried about how to play. Mrs. Smith suggests that just the two of them practice first. Jonathan likes this idea. Mrs. Smith pretends to be the child who wants to play kickball and enacts a scenario in which she approaches a group of children and asks, "Could I play, too?" She instructs Jonathan to play the role of one of the other children and helps him respond by saying, "Sure." Mrs. Smith then tells Jonathan, "Now would you like to try asking?" Jonathan then role-plays, asking to play kickball. Mrs. Smith pretends to be a child who welcomes him to play the game, and she sets out some chairs to be bases so that Jonathan can practice kicking the ball and playing the game.

Offering children on the autism spectrum an opportunity to rehearse play skills helps a child remember what to do in certain situations. The role-play should occur with someone whom the child knows and trusts so that he feels comfortable with trying out something new and potentially making a mistake. By practicing a given task in a low-pressure situation and performing the steps of that task in advance, the child gains clear expectations of what he needs to do when he tries the activity on his own. He can develop a sense of competence before interacting directly with peers as he comes to recognize that he is capable of joining them in a game or other type of play. By practicing and role-playing, the child knows what to expect and gains confidence in his own abilities, thereby reducing his anxiety and setting him up for success in peer-based play.

If the overall goal is to help a child find enjoyment and success while playing with peers, it's important to remember that the demands of the social setting should not overwhelm him. The idea is to stretch play skills slowly and to focus on helping the child self-regulate if he becomes agitated or upset. It's easy to lose sight of self-regulation by getting caught up in a game or activity and becoming focused on finishing it. If a child becomes dysregulated, it's best to discontinue the play at least temporarily because the play session can't be engaging and productive if the child is overwhelmed. It's therefore key that as facilitators we make sure to promote self-regulation when implementing the strategies discussed in this chapter.

Whether we're facilitating group play, previewing the rules of a game, or practicing for an upcoming event with peers, we must work to ensure that children feel security even as they move out of their comfort zone to play with other children. As part I of this book makes clear, *self-regulation always takes priority over teaching new skills,* for a child is not capable of mastering new skills or internalizing new lessons when he is in a state of emotional distress. Of course, there are times when children show resistance to learning the play skills we seek to instill. As the next chapter shows, there are ways that we can help children overcome their hesitation and attempts at avoidance without leading them down a path of anxiety and dysregulation.

13

MAINTAINING PLAY AND
COPING WITH RESISTANCE

Children on the autism spectrum frequently lack motivation and confidence when it comes to play. Because of these feelings, children may show apparent disinterest in playing with others and seek to avoid the "fun" activities, events, and interactions that their peers greatly enjoy. But as we have seen, this disengagement is not necessarily a sign that a child is indifferent to play. Minimizing social interaction is a common mechanism that autistic children use to cope with painful feelings that arise from anxiety and uncertainty about the unwritten rules of play. Let's turn now to explore strategies that are effective not only for teaching play skills when children seem disengaged, but also for managing the strong emotions that emerge when children show resistance to our efforts at engaging them in play.

Mrs. Smith sits down with Jonathan in the play kitchen, where she finds him sitting at a little table staring into the corner of the room. She says, "I'm hungry. I think there are some cookies around here. Have you seen them?" She sees the play cookies nearby and pretends to eat them. Jonathan continues to look away. She adds, "These are delicious! Would you like to try them?" She offers him a cookie. He looks at it but does not take it. She tries again, saying, "Oh, would you rather have something else? I think there's some strawberries over here." Still no response.

She grabs a Yoda doll, because she knows Jonathan loves Star Wars. She speaks in her best Yoda voice, "I'll have some strawberries. I'm starving." At this point, Jonathan looks at Yoda and smiles. Mrs. Smith holds Yoda up to face Jonathan and speaks in her Yoda voice, "Hey, Jonathan, what else is there good to eat around here?" Jonathan takes the Yoda figure and feeds him some cookies.

In this scene Mrs. Smith successfully overcomes Jonathan's initial reluctance to play, and she develops a lively imaginative scenario to gain his attention and engagement. When attempting to play with a child who is on the autism spectrum, don't be surprised or offended if you are at first met with apparent disinterest or indifference. Do not be discouraged if the child doesn't make eye contact, moves away from you, and seems hesitant to engage. Keep in mind that the child has probably had many experiences in which he has felt incompetent, anxious, or humiliated in social interactions and play situations. Slowly building positive play experiences increases a child's self-esteem and self-confidence, encouraging him to be more open to interactions with peers.

Here are some strategies to deal with a child's potential resistance, avoidance, or difficulty in maintaining play.

- *Persist.* If the child walks away, looks away, or seems disinterested, do not give up. Be persistent. Seek to gain the child's attention in an enticing manner. Include something in the play that appeals to the child's interests and passions, as Mrs. Smith does when she has Yoda ask Jonathan if there is anything to eat.

  In this case, she finds a play object that might grab Jonathan's attention. If the child moves away from the play, redirect him by announcing, in a matter-of-fact way, what has been left unfinished. For example, to continue the play, Mrs. Smith can say, "Oh no! We haven't fed C-3PO. We can't leave him hungry!" This type of remark might encourage the child to stick with the play scheme a little bit longer.

- *Insist on a response.* Children on the autism spectrum often do not respond to questions asked of them. They might appear as if they are ignoring you or do not hear you. Do not be offended if a child does not respond to you, but also do not accept being ignored. Keep asking the question in multiple ways, creatively using different objects and toys to encourage interaction and engagement. Use animation and excitement to stimulate interest. Use gestures and body language in an exaggerated way to gain the child's attention. Try to view a child's lack of responsiveness as a challenge that allows you to be creative in figuring out what sparks his interest and engagement.

- *Play dumb.* This is a great way to rope in a seemingly disinterested child because this strategy enables him to feel competent and successful as he enters a play scheme. Present a problem for the child to solve. Pretend you do not know how to do something. Act confused, bewildered, and concerned. Make a plea for help. You might say, for example, "Oh no! The bear can't find his family. What should we do?" During pretend play there are many opportunities to play dumb, allowing the child to feel capable and helpful.

- *Expand on the child's interests and life experiences.* Whenever possible, integrate the child's passions, interests, and life experiences into your interaction with him in order to promote engagement. Mrs. Smith chooses to use *Star Wars* figures because she knows Jonathan loves *Star Wars.* You can also include family pets, family members, places of interest, favorite toys, movies, and activities. The sky is the limit in terms of incorporating relevant material into the play.

- *Provide meaning to the child's actions.* Make interpretations and discuss the child's intentions as you play in order to add meaning, purpose, and function to the play. Discuss what is happening by saying, for example, "Wow, it's a good thing we found some food for C-3PO. He must have been starving. I wonder what else he wants to eat."

- *Make the wrong move.* Purposefully do the wrong thing to get the child's attention. For example, put the wrong piece in a puzzle, feed the wrong thing to the baby doll, or give the wrong answer to a question. Many children on the autism spectrum think very concretely and have a need for things to be complete, finished, and correct. Making the wrong move may refocus their attention, giving them a way into a play scheme or social interaction.

- *Playful obstruction.* Purposefully mess things up to redirect a child's attention when she is having difficulty maintaining play. Create a scenario in which some aspect of the play is disrupted so that the child can remedy the situation. The goal is not to mess things up to the point at which the child gets upset, but rather to create a moderate obstruction that prompts her to engage in order to resolve the issue. For example, after laying railroad tracks, pretend to mess them up accidentally so that they need to be put back together. Have the vehicles get in a pretend accident so that they need to be fixed. Or at a tea party, pretend to knock down all the cups accidentally so that they need to be put back on the table.

- *Add sensory input.* Though we discuss this topic further in the next section, adding sensory input such as jumping, singing, and swinging can help stimulate the child and enable him to refocus on the play scheme at hand. Children on the autism spectrum have a tendency to overreact or underreact to environmental stimuli such as sights, smells, sounds, and physical touch. Therefore, we must work to help them feel "just right" so that their nervous system maintains the proper level of arousal.

If a child seems understimulated—that is, if he seems tired, bored, or sullen, try offering him a large exercise ball for bouncing as you engage him in play. Sing a song involving physical activity such as "Heads, Shoulders, Knees, and Toes," or play a game with movement like hide-and-seek. Even the simple act of changing your tone of voice may be helpful in stimulating a child and keeping him engaged in play. Use a more excited tone, mimic the voice of a familiar character, or make noises imitating animals, trains, or other things relevant to the play scheme.

For an overstimulated child who can't maintain play because he is "bouncing off the walls," the approach is just the opposite. Speak in soft tones, dim the lights, and lower the music or any other ambient noise if possible. Gain his attention by using touch to give the child gentle squeezes or a back scratch. Direct him to calming play activities that involve tactile materials such as Play-Doh, sand, or paint. To keep autistic children engaged in play, we need to help regulate their nervous systems by modulating the level of activity as necessary.

RESISTANCE

Accept that resistance is common and normal in developing play with autistic children. Remember that we are asking them to do something that feels unfamiliar, uncomfortable, and anxiety provoking. If the child does not want to join in, do not be discouraged. Children need time to adjust to new challenges. Keep playing and keep modeling! It's equally important to be aware of your own feelings. Recognize especially when you are getting frustrated, anxious, or upset. These feelings powerfully affect autistic children, who often seem to absorb the anxiety of those around them like a sponge. This shared sense of anxiety only leads them to become more resistant to the idea of playing.

Be prepared for autistic children to express harsh feelings to you in moments of resistance. Do not react in anger. Instead, use their strong response as a teaching moment to promote skills of self-regulation:

- Label their feelings by saying, "You seem angry."
- Give feedback by telling them, "It hurts my feelings when you use mean words."
- Set limits by briefly reminding them, "Keep your hands to yourself and use your words."

- Teach coping skills by declaring, "Let's go to your break spot. It's good to take a break when we are upset."

It's fine for you to take a break, too. Model walking away when upset.

THE TAKEAWAY

Children on the autism spectrum often do not develop play skills in the same way that their neurotypical peers do. Fortunately, however, there are many effective strategies that can be implemented to teach autistic children how to play—an activity that both promotes a child's development and builds self-regulation skills in the long term. As the previous chapters show in detail, the following points are key when it comes to teaching autistic children play skills.

Play Skills Challenges	Strategies to Teach Play Skills
• Egocentric play and limited theory of mind • Difficulty with reciprocity, sharing, turn taking, and losing • Delayed development of pretend play • Slower processing of verbal information, social cues, and the multiple messages of play • Little intrinsic motivation for play • Lack of acceptance by neurotypical children	• Follow the child's lead and get on his level • Expand on the play, describe what's happening in the play, join in, and act like a kid • Video record play • Designate a play partner • Preview play scenarios and practice beforehand • Maintain play through resistance and creative redirection

Once we see the reasons why autistic children have difficulty with play, we can understand why they are often unmotivated by peer interaction. Playing with other children—whether in imaginative scenarios or more formal games—is an intimidating prospect that often feels unpredictable and chaotic for children on the spectrum. Given that many autistic children are unsuccessful in their initial attempts at play, we can also see why they may choose to stay on the sidelines and avoid the activities and interactions that neurotypical children often delight in.

If we implement the strategies described in part IV of this book, we can ease children into the world of imaginative and peer-based play, providing support and structure that will help them to be successful as they interact with their classmates, siblings, and friends. It is important that we actively work to develop the play skills of autistic children because play offers them numerous opportunities for social and emotional growth. When children play, for example, they exercise their imaginations. Through the act of pretending, they learn to see things from different perspectives. During play they also practice flexibility by sharing, taking turns, and learning to accept that everyone sometimes loses at games. In all these ways, play is crucial for promoting coping skills and the capacity for self-regulation. In part V, we focus on another topic that is central to promoting self-regulation in autistic children—managing sensory processing issues.

V

MAKING SENSE OF THE SENSES

We all take in and respond to information from our senses. We organize and interpret sensations from our bodies and our environment. This is called sensory processing. Children on the autism spectrum frequently have sensory processing challenges. This means that they struggle to feel "just right." Let's look at an example of this problem.

Three-year-old Cole found trips to the beach both exhilarating and annoying. Just getting ready for the beach was hard. When his father put sunscreen on him, Cole yelled that the lotion was too cold, and Cole hit his father when he tried to rub the sunscreen on his face. Walking out to the beach was challenging, as well, because Cole hated the feeling of the hot sand against his feet. Other people stared as Cole screamed that it felt like needles were stabbing him. But when he finally got to the water, Cole loved the sensation of the waves pounding against his body. He

Children with sensory processing disorder struggle to feel "just right."

stayed in the water for more than an hour, not talking or engaging with anyone as he let the waves crash against him again and again. When his parents thought that Cole needed a break, they escorted him out of the water and suggested that he sit down and have a snack. But Cole refused and shouted that he was done with the beach. Cole couldn't focus on anything except the sensation of his wet bathing suit, which was clinging to his body, making him feel constricted, and dripping water down his legs. Even though there were other people all around him on the beach, Cole suddenly yanked his swimsuit down and kicked it off. His parents moved quickly to cover Cole with a towel then packed up their stuff and headed back to the car, feeling anxious and disappointed about having to end their beach day much earlier than expected.

In this scenario, Cole has difficulty with self-regulation because he struggles to manage the many forms of sensory input that he experiences at the beach. Cole is averse to the way that the cold sunscreen, hot sand, and wet bathing suit make him feel. Although most people would agree that these sensations are uncomfortable, they prove to be completely intolerable for Cole as a child on the autism spectrum. Unable to modulate his response to the sensory stimuli he experiences, Cole has outbursts of anger, aggression, and impulsive behavior. However, at the same time that he feels a strong aversion to some sensations at the beach, Cole also shows signs of being a sensory "seeker" as well. For example, he likes the way that the crashing waves and the pressure of the water feel against his body. During the time he spends in the water, Cole fixates on these sensations; the comfort he derives from this sensory input overrides his interest in social engagement and other beach activities.

Cole's experiences at the beach offer a glimpse into the sensory processing challenges frequently seen in children on the autism spectrum. These challenges are a sign of what is known as sensory processing disorder, a condition that interferes with the way we organize, interpret, and respond to the information we take in through our senses.

Sensory processing disorder is considered to be a common component of autism—one that often proves to be a great source of strife for autistic children. Their experience of the world often swings between modes of heightened and lowered sensitivity to environmental stimuli. Because many autistic children struggle to manage extreme reactions to a barrage of different sensations, sensory processing issues are often at the root of their difficulties with self-regulation.

> **Sensory processing disorder is a condition that interferes with the way we organize, interpret, and respond to the information taken in through the senses.**

WHAT IS SENSORY PROCESSING DISORDER?

All people experience sensory processing problems on some level. Perhaps you have felt annoyed by an itchy tag on the back of your shirt, or maybe you have found certain textures or smells to be extremely bothersome. You might also think of a time when you felt ill at ease because you were at a loud party, you were on a bumpy airplane ride, or you had a nagging headache. Undoubtedly, in these situations you found yourself struggling to moderate some of the sensations you were feeling, perhaps actively seeking a way to minimize your discomfort. However, for people who have sensory processing disorder, everyday circumstances can be a source of significant distress and anxiety.

Sensory processing disorder involves a problem with the central nervous system in detecting, organizing, and responding to information perceived through the senses. Recent research on the disorder shows that there are altered tracts of white matter in the brains of children who have sensory processing difficulties. This neurological variation results in impaired communication between the different parts of the brain responsible for assessing, interpreting, and organizing sensory information (Yi Shin et al., 2016).

One analogy sometimes used to illustrate this problem is to imagine that the brain has a traffic jam. As a person receives input through the senses, the messages that the brain receives and sends may get misinterpreted or rerouted. This miscommunication can make it difficult for people to distinguish one sensation from another and to modulate their reactions to environmental stimuli. Sensory processing problems also affect the ability to plan an action in response to the information perceived through the senses. Although there is no known cause of sensory processing disorder, environmental factors, prenatal and birth complications, and genetic histories seem to influence the development of the disorder (Kranowitz, 2005).

For children especially, sensory processing difficulties have a major impact on their behavior and learning (Kranowitz, 2005). The self-regulation challenges that autistic children experience often stem from the challenges they face in modulating their responses to sensory input. Sometimes these children are bothered by stimuli that neurotypical people barely notice, and this over-responsiveness can result in feelings of annoyance, discomfort, and outright aggression. At other times, they are under-responsive to environmental stimuli. In this case, they might have low energy levels and appear lethargic or disengaged; alternatively, they might seek out the sensory input that their bodies crave by engaging in self-stimulatory behaviors such as running back and forth or walking in circles.

It's important to remember that all people, including those with sensory processing disorder, perceive sensations differently. We organize, interpret, and react to environmental stimuli in our own unique ways (Reebye & Stalker, 2010). Therefore, what is pleasurable to one person may be upsetting to another. Moreover, even within a short time frame, an autistic child might find himself experiencing a strong aversion to some sensations while seeking input from others. However, what unites all people with sensory processing disorder is the fact that they experience significant dysregulation and disruption in everyday life as a result of difficulties in perceiving and responding to information taken in through the senses.

When it comes to helping children with sensory issues, we certainly recommend that they participate in occupational therapy, which offers treatments that specifically target the symptoms of sensory processing disorder. One important intervention that occupational therapists can make is to design a "sensory diet," which is an individualized routine of activities developed to help a child feel "just right" throughout the day. A sensory diet has nothing to do with food, but it does offer a "menu" of activities that fulfills a child's need for stimulation and input from a variety of sources. A range of sensory-based activities and modes of play are woven into a child's day to help him focus and feel calm. A sensory diet usually includes some combination of activities that involve focus and attention, practice with fine and gross motor skills, and opportunities for relaxation.

Though the input of an occupational therapist is key in addressing sensory processing issues, it's also important to recognize that there are many easy ways that teachers and parents can help autistic children manage sensory challenges on a daily basis. By giving these children the right supports, we can reduce the negative impact of sensory processing disorder, increase their coping skills, and promote their overall capacity for self-regulation.

In the chapters that follow, we explore the sensory issues that commonly affect children with autism. We first explain the basics of the sensory system and outline the signs of sensory processing disorder. We then turn to present examples of three children with different sensory profiles, and we provide techniques for addressing specific types of sensory processing challenges. Because many children show signs of sensory processing disorder that cross these different profiles, we also offer a series of general strategies for use at home or school, which can alleviate a wide range of sensory difficulties that autistic children experience.

14

THE EIGHT SENSES

As children, we all learned about our five senses, which give us the ability to touch, taste, smell, hear, and see. However, it's quite possible that no one ever talked about the other three sensory systems in the human body. These include the proprioceptive system, the vestibular system, and the interoceptive system. Because we need to be familiar with all eight of the senses in order to understand the basics of sensory processing, let's turn now to explore these lesser-known sensory systems, which play an essential role in our daily lives by influencing everything from our physical movements to our emotional states.

Proprioception is the sensory system that controls our muscle and joint movements. This sense enables us to perceive the position of different parts of our bodies in relation to one another, and it makes us aware of the intensity of our movements. Proprioception allows us to move and control our limbs without looking at them, and in this regard, it is essential to activities that involve hand-eye coordination. For example, we rely on our proprioceptive system when we drive, an activity that requires looking at the road while simultaneously using our arms and feet to steer and control the vehicle's speed. Playing the piano is another activity that shows the proprioceptive system at work; a pianist must strike combinations of keys with varying intensity while also using his eyes to read sheet music. Bumping into others is commonly seen with children who have proprioception challenges because their sense of where their body is in space is compromised.

Working in tandem with the proprioceptive system is the vestibular system. Located in the inner ear, the receptors of the vestibular system are responsible for both the sensation of balance and the awareness of our body position. The vestibular system is activated when we engage in physical movements that challenge our sense of equilibrium. For example, the vestibular sense is what enables us to manage the strong sensations that result from movements like swinging or spinning, and it also allows us to regain a feeling of steadiness in the wake of these movements. When it comes to more routine activities in daily life, the vestibular system also plays an important role in helping us maintain physical stability. For example, when we are in the shower rinsing shampoo out of our hair by closing our eyes and tilting our heads back, it's the vestibular system that enables us to feel secure and stay balanced in this position.

Interoception, the third of the lesser-known senses, controls sensations that occur inside the body such as hunger, temperature, pain, and the need to go to the bathroom. Interoception enables the brain to process information from the body's internal organs so that we can be aware of both our physiological and emotional states. The interoceptive system is working, for example, when we recognize that we feel thirsty and then respond to this feeling by getting a drink. If we are in a stressful situation and our heart is beating fast, it is the interoceptive system that enables us to recognize this bodily sensation and to connect it with feelings of anxiety or fear. As the system that communicates messages about the body's internal equilibrium, interoception is key for maintaining self-regulation.

HOW SENSORY PROCESSING DISORDER AFFECTS THE EIGHT SENSES

Sensory processing disorder affects all of the senses, making it difficult for people to understand and engage with the world around them. When it comes to the five major senses, the effects of sensory processing disorder are relatively straightforward. For example, the disorder can cause tactile defensiveness, leading some people to recoil at being touched; however, these same people might also seek different forms of tactile input and enjoy the sensation of pressure and weight on their bodies. Because of sensory processing disorder, people may experience heightened sensitivity to certain textures, tastes, and smells. In some cases, sensory processing disorder can be associated with food aversion and extreme picky eating.

In terms of sight, the disorder often makes it difficult for people to find an object when other items are also present in their field of vision. Visual tracking—the ability to follow something with the eyes and to scan a line of text in reading—is also frequently impaired. Sensory processing disorder can affect hearing by making people either over-responsive or under-responsive to certain sounds. It can also interfere with auditory processing, making it hard for people to take in and respond to information that is presented verbally.

Sensory processing disorder also disrupts the proprioceptive, vestibular, and interoceptive systems. Because these are less familiar senses that prove to be essential to our daily functioning, let's look at an example showing how the disorder affects these sensory systems. As the following scenario demonstrates, people with autism often struggle with motor skills, coordination, and other movements controlled by the vestibular and proprioceptive senses. As we shall see, they also have decreased awareness of the body's internal sensations, making it harder for them to recognize messages from the interoceptive system signaling hunger, pain, body temperature, and the need use the bathroom (Fiene & Brownlow, 2015; Garfinkel et al., 2016).

During outside time on a hot day at preschool, Gabriela tries to climb a rock wall to get to the top of a play structure that is about four feet high. However, she can't figure out where to place her feet without looking directly at them, and she keeps slipping, banging her legs on the protruding footholds. After repeatedly kicking the rock wall in frustration, Gabriela eventually allows a teacher to help get her to the top of the play structure, where two other children are sitting.

When these kids decide to jump down to the ground, Gabriela attempts to follow suit, but she freezes. She is confused about how to coordinate her muscle movements, and she can't judge where her body is in relation to the ground. Her frustration quickly returns as she spends the next five minutes feeling torn between wanting to make the jump and not being sure if she can do it. During this period of increasingly agonizing indecision, the teacher announces that recess time is over. Gabriela feels extremely disappointed with herself as she finally resorts to getting help from the teacher once again to climb down from the top of the rock wall.

Although she needs a break because she is hot, sweaty, and thirsty by the end of recess, Gabriela does not register these sensations. Instead she becomes more irritable and gets in line feeling like she has missed the chance to do anything fun outside. When another student accidentally bumps into Gabriela as they head back to the classroom, she shouts at him and stomps on his foot.

Though it may not be obvious to the untrained eye, Gabriela's impulsive behavior ultimately stems from the mounting dysregulation she experiences due to sensory processing disorder. Her inability to climb to the top of the rock wall and then jump down is a sign that both her proprioceptive and vestibular systems are not functioning correctly. Gabriela also proves to be unaware of the signals being sent by her interoceptive system. Neurotypical people instinctively recognize the signs of becoming overheated and thirsty, but Gabriela does not perceive these sensations.

Throughout recess Gabriela also clearly has trouble planning actions that mark an effective response to the information she takes in through her senses. She can't climb the rock wall, and she ends up kicking it in frustration; she can't jump down from the play structure, and she ultimately freezes and struggles with anxiety; she can't recognize that she is hot and thirsty, and she becomes irritable and angry instead of cooling off and getting a drink. In all of these instances, Gabriela engages in a series of maladaptive reactions to the sensory input that she struggles to process and interpret. Her difficult behavior is driven by sensory needs that she can neither recognize nor fulfill on her own.

SENSORY THINKERS

We should not underestimate the impact of sensory issues on an autistic person's life because people on the autism spectrum tend to experience sensations more intensely than neurotypical people. They frequently process information taken in through their senses as raw data, whereas neurotypical people tend to process much of their sensory experience through language.

Language helps to mediate our encounters with the world; putting sensations and feelings into words helps us process and make sense of the data we take in through our senses. For example, when a neurotypical person gets into a hot car, he thinks, "I'm hot, but I know that the air conditioner will kick in and that I'll feel better soon." However, for many autistic children, such sensations feel overwhelming, and language doesn't work as an effective interpretive lens through which to process sensory information. Even when autistic children are highly verbal, their thinking is often shaped primarily by their raw sensory experience. This sensory-based mode of thinking is also frequently connected to strong emotions. As a result, for many children on the autism spectrum, a particular sensation or experience can make a lasting impression on them, influencing their perception of a specific place, activity, or object for months or even years to come (Nason, 2014).

Four-year-old Declan refuses to use the bathroom adjacent to his prekindergarten classroom. When he is in the yard, the cafeteria, or anywhere else at school, he will go to the bathroom without any problem. But when it's time to line up to use the bathroom nearest his classroom, he says he does not have to go. This is obviously not the case, however, and sometimes Declan has an accident if he falls asleep at rest time.

When his parents ask their son what's going on, Declan explains that earlier in the school year, he saw that there were paper towels all over the floor when he went to use the bathroom near his classroom. Knowing that their son can't stand the feeling of scratchy paper towels, Declan's parents realize that his sensory aversion is at the root of the problem. Even though the paper towels were cleaned up quickly and the floor has been clear ever since, Declan still refuses to go in the same bathroom months later. The strong sensations he felt in a single moment overpower his rational thinking, and he continues to perceive the bathroom as a contaminated space.

As this example shows, autistic children tend to be sensory thinkers, processing information and forming memories around sensory experiences. Memories are closely tied to sensations, and the strong impression of a past experience can override different circumstances in the present. It can be taxing for autistic children to try to translate sensory experiences into words. In the case of Declan, who is a very articulate child, he only offers an explanation at the gentle urging of his parents while at home, a place removed from the school space that causes him so much anxiety.

Children on the autism spectrum rely heavily on their sensory experiences in understanding their world. Quite often, something goes awry with their ability to process, interpret, and respond logically to the information they take in through their eight senses. When this happens, there are clear signs that a child is having sensory processing difficulties, and we turn to explore these signs in the next chapter.

15

SIGNS AND SYMPTOMS OF SENSORY PROCESSING CHALLENGES IN CHILDREN

Although we have touched on the ways that sensory processing disorder affects the eight senses, it is important to describe how the disorder generally manifests itself in children on the autism spectrum. Sensory processing problems may be apparent very early in a child's life, and children with sensory issues are often reputed to be colicky babies who have a difficult time sleeping and falling into any type of schedule. As they grow into toddlers, these children tend to be troubled by personal care activities such as washing hair, clipping fingernails, brushing teeth, and getting haircuts.

Appointments for the doctor and the dentist can also be challenging because these visits require children to tolerate a number of uncomfortable sensations and to accept the invasion of their personal space. For example, children with sensory issues might strongly resist having the inside of their ears or nose examined with the scope used by the doctor. Or they might not be able to bear the buzzing sound of the dentist's electric toothbrush and the gritty texture of the toothpaste on it.

FEELING "OUT OF SYNC"

Whereas routine activities at day care or preschool are likely to be less intrusive than the experiences described above, a child with sensory issues faces challenges in all aspects of life, demonstrating clear signs of sensory processing disorder. Carol Stock Kranowitz uses the term "out of sync" to describe children who struggle to process and respond to sensory information (2003). This descriptor is certainly broad, but it nonetheless encompasses a cohesive range of symptoms and behaviors indicating dysfunction in one or more of the body's eight senses. Offering a compilation of recent research on sensory issues, the following lists describe the common signs of sensory processing challenges in children.

When it comes to general reactions to environmental stimuli, children with sensory processing disorder may

- be overresponsive to touch, movement, sights, or sound;
- be under-responsive to touch, movement, sights, or sound;
- be unusually impulsive, fidgety, inattentive, and easily distracted; or
- have an unusually high level or low level of energy. (Reebye & Stalker, 2010)

There are also physical manifestations of sensory processing disorder, which impairs motor skills, coordination, and core muscle strength. In this regard, children with sensory challenges may

- have delayed development of gross motor skills such as running, jumping, and climbing;
- have delayed development of fine motor skills such as cutting with scissors and drawing;
- have poor motor planning and difficulty coordinating their bodies to perform an action;
- have poor oral-motor skills such as chewing and speaking;
- appear clumsy and have difficulty coordinating both sides of the body together;
- fatigue easily and have difficulty sitting erect, often slouching or sprawling on the floor;
- misjudge distances between themselves and other people or objects, perhaps trying to squeeze into a space that is too small or knocking into others while trying to move past them;
- have a poor sense of rhythm and timing; and
- have a poor sense of body awareness. (Reebye & Stalker, 2010)

Sensory processing disorder can also have cognitive and emotional effects, making it hard for a child to follow instructions and keep up with the changing activities of a busy day. It is not hard to imagine that children can become upset more easily when they struggle to process information, manage extreme responses to environmental stimuli, and move and coordinate their bodies efficiently. In this regard, when children have sensory processing disorder, they may

- respond slowly to verbal directions or become easily frustrated by verbal directions;
- become easily frustrated when their expectations aren't met;
- prefer sameness and a predictable routine;
- have difficulty with transitions;
- have difficulty regulating their mood; and
- have difficulty falling asleep at night. (Kranowitz, 2003)

As this information suggests, sensory processing problems interfere with a wide variety of skills and abilities that are essential to feeling successful and staying regulated in everyday life. For example, a child who finds it difficult to follow directions, to pay attention, and to perform fine motor tasks will have trouble succeeding from the beginning of his earliest years in school. A child who is over-responsive to the noise, lights, and smells in his classroom may have a complete meltdown when asked to do a seemingly fun activity simply because his emotional energy has been depleted in trying to manage the sensations that assail him. A child who is clumsy, who continually bumps into people, and who can't keep up with his peers in games like soccer or tag is likely to feel incompetent and to struggle with making friends. And, finally, a child who can't seem to control his emotions, who frustrates easily, and who has difficulty with transitions is likely to seem ill-behaved or even defiant when he is actually trying his best and wants to follow the rules. In all of these cases, children struggle on a day-to-day basis because of their sensory challenges. Their learning, behavior, emotional well-being, social skills, and physical development are all adversely affected by sensory processing disorder.

IDENTIFYING SENSORY PROCESSING ISSUES

Because sensory processing challenges affect so many aspects of a child's life, it's easy to mistake these issues for other problems or disorders that obscure the root cause of a child's difficulties. If one looks only at the superficial characteristics of a child's behavior, it is possible to confuse sensory processing disorder with a number of other diagnoses and conditions, including attention deficit hyperactivity disorder, oppositional defiant disorder, obsessive compulsive disorder, excessive fatigue, or depression (Reebye & Stalker, 2010).

Although sensory processing issues can certainly co-occur with other disorders and health problems, it's important to pay close attention to the reasons for a child's behavior, aiming to identify potential triggers that fall within the domain of sensory processing. For example, if a child frequently gets angry and teases her peers when she is at the art center, make sure to consider the sensory demands that the child must manage in this particular setting. Do the art materials have textures or smells that bother the child, possibly taxing her coping skills and draining her energy for appropriate social interaction? Are the child's fine motor skills delayed? Is she struggling with drawing, painting, or using scissors to the point that she feels inferior to the other children who readily produce artwork that looks much better than hers?

> We do a great disservice to autistic children when we assume that they have a psychological or behavioral disorder without thoroughly investigating the root causes of the difficulties they experience.

When we see that an autistic child is struggling with self-regulation and disruptive behavior, we need to think like detectives, looking for patterns and potentially elusive triggers that point to sensory processing issues. We do a great disservice to autistic children when we assume that they have a psychological or behavioral disorder without thoroughly investigating the root causes of the difficulties they experience.

There are some key observations about children's behavior that may help to clarify if sensory processing disorder is present. After watching the child over a period of time and after seeing him engaged in a number of different activities, consider the following questions:

- What is the child's level of alertness? Can the child maintain energy to stay engaged in an activity?
- Is the child's emotional tone appropriate to the activity?
- Does the child avoid new situations and have difficulty transitioning to different activities?
- How does the child respond to touch? Is he overly sensitive to activities that involve touching items? Or is he under-responsive to touch and engagement in sensory-driven activities?
- How does the child engage in movement activities? Is she uncoordinated or clumsy? Does she struggle with planning the movement of her body?
- Does the child have poor self-esteem and lack confidence?
- Does the child have poor social skills? (Isbell & Isbell, 2007; Williamson & Anzalone, 2001).

If you recognize the signs of sensory processing disorder, it's important to make purposeful interventions since these problems will not go away on their own. In addition to referring a child to an occupational therapist or a developmental pediatrician, there are many helpful strategies that parents and teachers can put in place on a day-to-day basis. These interventions are important because sensory processing disorder is not fundamentally a behavioral problem that can be managed with rewards and consequences or other conventional disciplinary approaches. As the next chapters show, we must implement the right supports to offset the impact of sensory processing problems, which can affect everything in a child's life from physical movement and coordination to social interaction and emotional regulation.

16

DOMINANT CLASSES OF SENSORY PROCESSING DISORDER

Profiles and Strategies

There are many manifestations of sensory processing problems that can be seen in both a child's behavior and his emotional response to the environment. Below we offer profiles of three different children to highlight the dominant classes of sensory processing disorder. We have intentionally crafted each profile to feature a cluster of related challenges so that parents and teachers can learn to differentiate among the wide range of signs that characterize sensory processing disorder.

Before we explore these profiles, however, it's important to acknowledge that not all children fit neatly into a single category. Most children, in fact, experience multiple challenges that cut across the different classes of the disorder (Williamson & Anzalone, 2001). Because every person's brain is unique, all children have distinctive sensory-processing abilities and challenges. Even within the same child, sensory processing can be remarkably variable, changing daily or even on a moment-to-moment basis. Let us therefore keep these important caveats in mind as we turn now to explore three distinct sensory profiles describing an over-responsive child, an under-responsive child, and a sensory-seeking child.

AN OVER-RESPONSIVE CHILD

A heightened sense of sounds, sights, and textures makes Hector averse to many activities and experiences.

Hector sits outside the group during circle time at preschool. He appears to be inattentive, fearful, and cautious. Though Hector usually chooses not to engage in class-wide activities, today he agrees to be the leader who assembles the calendar. As he walks up to the front of the classroom, Hector bumps into several children who are seated on the floor and steps on someone's finger. When he stands next to the teacher, he feels nervous because he has never been at the front of the class before, and he does not like to be in new situations.

The teacher instructs Hector to put various pieces into plastic slots on the calendar marking the day of the week, the date, and the weather. Hector seems confused about how to assemble the calendar even though he has seen it done many times. When the teacher realizes that he is having trouble sorting the calendar pieces, she puts her hand on Hector's back to offer him reassurance, but he quickly pulls away from her touch. The children try to help by calling out directions, but Hector feels like they are rushing him, and they make him feel dumb. Their voices are also loud, and Hector ends up covering his ears and standing like a statue, overwhelmed by all of the stimulation.

Hector exhibits classic signs of sensory processing disorder with over-responsiveness. He is anxious, cautious, and highly reactive to stimuli in the environment. Because these children have overreactive nervous systems, they frequently attempt to reduce the amount of stimulation they experience. As a result, these over-responsive children rarely show excitement, and sometimes they might even appear to be sullen. But this apparent lack of engagement is not necessarily a sign of their personality or disinterest in social interaction. Rather, the flat affect sometimes seen in over-responsive children stems from their attempt to avoid becoming overwhelmed by the stimuli they experience so acutely. They seek to minimize the feelings of discomfort and anxiety that arise when they take in sensory information (Williamson & Anzalone, 2001).

As Hector's experience makes clear, over-responsive children struggle with sensory input in numerous ways, and they have trouble in situations with lots of sounds, movement, and visual stimulation. Walking to the front of the classroom, for example, Hector bumps into his peers, showing that he lacks awareness of his body position in a crowded space. Even though he possesses above-average intelligence, Hector exhibits difficulty with visual discrimination and motor planning. It is clear that he struggles to organize the multiple parts of the calendar task when he can't readily distinguish among the pieces and place them in the correct pockets. Hector also recoils at an unpredictable touch and retreats from loud sounds. His attempt at assembling the calendar develops into a situation that ultimately overtaxes his cognitive and emotional resources. Instead of asking for help or trying to finish the task, Hector eventually shuts down and refuses to participate in the activity.

It is possible to misinterpret Hector's response to the calendar activity as an instance of avoidant or noncompliant behavior. If the teacher were to take this perspective and insist that Hector complete the calendar task, the situation would only degenerate, increasing the likelihood of Hector having a major temper tantrum. It's important to recognize that Hector abruptly disengages because he is overwhelmed with sensory information and feelings of incompetence. In this instance, he needs support and understanding, not increased demands. We must therefore be mindful of the clues showing that Hector's primary difficulty is with processing, organizing, and responding to the information he takes in through his senses.

STRATEGIES FOR THE OVER-RESPONSIVE CHILD

We must remember that an autistic child is doing his best to manage the multitude of sensory input he perceives. A certain experience or encounter—something that is potentially imperceptible to others—might be the proverbial straw that broke the camel's back for an over-responsive child. Sensory experiences gradually lead to the accumulation of stress and anxiety, and a

Sensory input is cumulative and becomes overwhelming for the over-responsive child.

child may not yet have the coping skills to manage these negative feelings. But there are strategies that can help minimize sensory difficulties for over-responsive children and teach them how to cope.

Decrease Sensory Overload

Over-responsive children struggle to organize their environment, to plan their motor activities, and to understand and interpret multiple stimuli from their senses. We can help by consciously shaping and structuring the environment around them (Reebye & Stalker, 2010; Williamson & Anzalone, 2001). Returning to the example of Hector, we can see that there are many ways to modify the setting so that sensory issues do not become an obstacle to his successful participation in the calendar activity.

To ease motor planning difficulties, make a clear path so that children can come to the front of the room without having to navigate around many small bodies. Reduce other forms of stimulation as well. Instruct the other children to sit as quietly as possible in order to minimize noise and encourage them to be patient and to give their classmates time to complete a task without shouting out directions or answers. Also do your best to avoid engaging in unpredictable movements or touches that might provoke anxiety in over-responsive children like Hector. With these simple modifications, Hector's sensory system is better able to interpret and organize the stimulation from the environment.

Modify the Task

When Hector approaches the calendar, his visual field is a blur. He sees many rows of plastic pockets and a jumble of pieces featuring different words, numbers, and pictures. This busy facade of information overwhelms Hector's visual processing abilities, and he struggles to organize the different pieces and position them correctly on the calendar.

To help Hector in this situation, we can break the task into smaller steps, beginning first with the date, then the day of the week, and then the weather. Give him one piece at a time and point to the place on the calendar where it goes. By minimizing the clutter in his visual field and offering one-step directions, Hector can complete the task successfully because his motor planning and visual processing abilities are not overtaxed. Addressing the core sensory issues enables him to use his intelligence and problem-solving skills. Hector now feels comfortable completing the task, and his self-confidence blossoms.

Prepare for Sensory Challenges: More Previewing!

Because over-responsive children can feel overwhelmed and distressed by seemingly ordinary sensations and activities, we can emphasize predictability to give them a sense of control in an environment that often feels overpowering to them. These children become anxious quickly when called on to complete a task for which they feel unprepared. They like to know when something is going to happen and what exactly will take place.

In our example with Hector, the teacher could prepare him for the challenging activity by letting him know before circle time that it's his turn to assemble the calendar. With this information, Hector can begin the work of processing the parts of the task before he finds himself put on the spot, standing in front of the class. Giving Hector advance notice also becomes an opportunity for the teacher to reassure him that she will be right there to help him with every step so that he knows that nothing can go wrong. Allowing time to prepare and establishing a sense of routine and repetition are key resources for helping over-responsive children develop a sense of confidence and mastery over challenging sensory stimuli.

AN UNDER-RESPONSIVE CHILD

With a muted response to environmental stimuli, Sophie is slow to interact with others and engage in activities.

Sophie is quiet and frequently disengaged. She is less interactive than her peers, and she often looks bored and inattentive. One morning at preschool, the children are excited because their teacher has brought in a new book and game about dinosaurs. When the teacher begins reading the interactive story, the children get involved by repeating the names of the dinosaurs they learn about and by practicing a special move associated with each dinosaur. As her peers have fun tiptoeing like T. rexes and twisting like pteranodons, Sophie lies on the floor at a remove from everyone else and stares out the window.

When the story is over, the teacher brings out a large spinner with pictures of the dinosaurs on it, and she explains that when the spinner lands on a specific dinosaur, the children should do the move that they have learned to associate with it. The teacher asks Sophie to stand up and join the class, but she does not respond and remains near the window as the game begins.

Although Sophie has heard both the teacher's instructions and the dinosaur story, she doesn't reply because she can't organize a response quickly enough. She also struggles to understand the directions of the game and to remember all the different movements involved. Sophie is overwhelmed by information that her classmates readily process. As a result, she feels tired and loses interest in the game. She remains on the sidelines watching the other children, and as she does this, she engages repeatedly in spinning her body.

Sophie displays common signs of sensory processing disorder with under-responsiveness. Her sensory system is slow to take in and interpret stimuli from the environment. She also struggles to enact a response to sensory information. Sophie is less interactive with others, and she therefore struggles to socialize, play, and engage in structured group activities.

Even though her peers are enjoying a lively game, she seems disinterested and bored. Like the over-responsive child, then, Sophie's affect is restricted, but for different reasons. The under-responsive child appears disengaged not because she is trying to avoid uncomfortable sensations, but because she needs more stimulation to help jump-start her sensory responses. Under-responsive children like Sophie experience the world in a state of low arousal. They tend to be less reactive to the sensory input they receive.

STRATEGIES FOR UNDER-RESPONSIVE CHILDREN

As is true for over-responsive children, it's easy to misinterpret the behavior of under-responsive children who can appear to be withdrawn or who might seem completely dismissive of any adult directive. Sometimes these children look like they are depressed because they tend to isolate themselves and have low energy, showing little interest in the world around them. In some cases, people restrict their interactions with under-responsive children because they can seem so removed. But what these children really need is *more* interaction and engagement with people who show excitement and enthusiasm.

Under-responsive children need increased stimulation to "amp up" their under-aroused sensory system (Williamson & Anzalone, 2001). Some of these children seek this sensory input on their own by engaging in self-stimulating activities such as spinning or pacing. It is important to remember that this behavior is not a sign of inattention or noncompliance. Adults can help promote the under-responsive child's engagement and increase her arousal level by encouraging such vigorous activity, interacting with the child in an animated way, and incorporating the following strategies.

Model Active Engagement

If we return to the example of Sophie, we can see that she is significantly under-aroused and under-stimulated by the new game being presented. She does not see why the other children are so excited because she struggles to take in the information that is presented, and she does not fully understand how to play the dinosaur game. Recognizing that sensory processing issues cause Sophie's disengagement, the teacher takes Sophie by the hand and says in an excited tone, "Let's try this game together!" Hand in hand, she helps Sophie spin the spinner. She then calls out the name of the dinosaur it lands on, and she reminds the class of the specific movement they need to do.

In this way, the teacher calls attention to each step of the game and models active participation for Sophie. Sophie sees her teacher's smile, hears her excited voice, and sees her enthusiastic actions. This helps to stimulate Sophie's sensory system, and she attempts to follow along in the game. If Sophie starts to lose focus, the teacher looks for fun ways to prompt her engagement. For example, she gives Sophie a "pteranodon tickle" at one point. At another point, she does something funny by falling down when it's her turn to jump as a dinosaur.

Increase Energy without Overstimulating

We want to provide stimulating activities in a controlled way to help children achieve and maintain an optimal level of arousal and attention. We can increase engagement in a subtle yet effective manner by using the sense of touch, perhaps taking the child's hand, as the teacher does in our example with Sophie. It can also be helpful to rub the child's back or to gently squeeze her shoulders, gestures that offer sensory input and reassurance at the same time. When children are in a state of low arousal, increase motor activity by walking, jumping, swinging, or climbing, depending on what is appropriate for the environment and circumstances. Be enthusiastic and use an excited tone of voice to entice more reaction from the child. Give under-responsive children the increased stimulation that they need by amplifying your emotions, interactions, and movements.

We want to spark the child's engagement in a friendly, energetic way without being overbearing. The goal is to energize the child's sensory system so that she will feel alert and interested in the activity at hand. We do not want to overwhelm the child inadvertently and lead her into the opposite extreme of becoming overstimulated. It is therefore important to watch carefully for the child's reaction. When she begins to respond and interact, we know that we are helping her sensory system to adapt. Assess how much stimulation the child can tolerate without becoming upset or overwhelmed. We need to be aware of signs that the child is getting too excited and reaching a point at which she might begin to shut down.

Provide Sensory Input

There are many ways to stimulate under-responsive children so that they feel "just right." We can consciously rev up sensory input through sound, movement, and touch. In our interactions with under-responsive children, for example, we should make sure to vary the pitch and intensity of our voices to convey the appropriate tone and level of energy (Isbell & Isbell, 2007). We can include music in the daily routine and give children opportunities to sing, dance, and play small instruments, such as a tambourine. During these activities it's helpful to incorporate movement whenever possible, perhaps when singing songs such as "The Wheels on the Bus."

If we create obstacle courses and play games like Simon Says, we also stimulate children's sensory systems and help them plan their physical movements in structured ways. In addition, we can promote their ability to organize sensory information by making the smallest of adjustments to ensure, for example, that their feet rest firmly on the floor or on a step stool when doing seated work at a desk or table. We can also help children focus by placing a strip of Velcro under the desk that they can rub with their hands to get sensory input when necessary.

The following list provides other easy techniques for stimulating the nervous system in under-responsive children. Offer them opportunities to

- sit on an exercise ball so they can bounce;
- sit on a Howda chair during group time or circle time for increased support of core muscles (rather than sitting on the floor with their legs crossed);
- sit in a child-sized chair with armrests (provides support and clearly defined boundaries, so the child does not sprawl out on floor);
- wear a weighted vest (if recommended by an occupational therapist);
- hold a hand fidget (TheraPutty, small toy, squishy ball);
- move around (run an errand, do a small job, serve as a helper, carry something heavy);
- engage in gross motor activities (running, walking, climbing, jumping, swinging);
- chew crunchy foods, bite on a specially designed chew tool, or suck liquid through a straw; or
- listen to music.

Since under-responsive children frequently prefer to sit on the sidelines and minimize interaction, it's important to support these children in an effort to increase their level of engagement. It is also important to allow under-responsive children extra time to warm up and react, as they tend to process information more slowly than their neurotypical peers. Under-responsive children might find an activity more appealing if a peer initiates social interaction and offers to help by demonstrating the steps of a task.

Make Play Enticing

Under-responsive children often have trouble organizing their bodies and cognitive faculties in response to stimuli. This difficulty can make play and other related activities feel more challenging than fun for these children. As is the case with Sophie, under-responsive children need increased structure, stimulation, and prompts to engage in play. Sophie's teacher approaches her with warmth and enthusiasm. Her energy feels contagious, and her silliness during the dinosaur game keeps Sophie engaged and amused despite her earlier refusal to participate.

In less structured moments of playtime, it's worth the effort to encourage under-responsive children to interact and have fun. For example, if a child likes Mr. Potato Head, bring that toy to him. If he seems disinterested at first, amp up the energy by making Mr. Potato Head talk, sing, jump, or tickle. Have him say, "Help me, help, I need my eyes! Have you seen my eyes?" This attitude of increased excitement encourages the child to participate in the game. Soon, he is smiling and showing interest in finding more pieces to help build Mr. Potato Head.

At this point, you can label feelings and reactions as a way to lend structure to the play. For example, you might say to the child, "Mr. Potato Head is so happy you have found his eyes! He's so glad you are helping him. You look happy, too." The technique of labeling emotions helps children organize their responses to sensory information and builds skills of self-regulation. Narrating the action of the play scenario also helps organize the task and sum up the interaction for the child. You might say to him, for example, "Putting Mr. Potato Head back together was so fun."

Play can be more engaging for under-responsive children if we use playful obstruction. Described in chapter 13, this technique involves presenting a problem for the child to solve as a way to spark interest and engagement. Playful obstruction works well for under-responsive children because creating a challenge motivates them to participate, offering an incentive that overrides their tendency to remain in a state of low arousal.

For example, the adult might deliberately put Mr. Potato Head's mouth in upside down and then say in a garbled voice, "Something seems to be wrong with my mouth. I can't make my lips and teeth work. And I'm hungry for a snack, but how can I eat anything like this? Oh, no." After seeing the problem, the child is driven to act by offering a solution, and it's likely that he will put Mr. Potato Head's mouth in the right position and perhaps do other funny things of his own with the pieces.

Increasing stimulation for the under-responsive child frequently challenges us to act childlike. Pretend you are the same age as the child with whom you are playing. Be silly, crawl on the floor, and exaggerate your emotions. This lively behavior will help to arouse and engage the under-responsive child. Encourage other peers to come over and join the fun.

A SENSORY-SEEKING CHILD

Brian is child who looks for more stimulation in order to feel comfortable.

Brian always seems to be on the move. He has difficulty sitting still when he is doing a craft or other work at the table in his preschool classroom. He frequently moves his body around in his chair, sometimes sitting on his legs, sometimes kneeling on his chair, sometimes standing up and sitting down repeatedly. At circle time, he squirms around continually instead of sitting cross-legged on the floor, and he frequently touches the other children and invades their space.

Brian has difficulty paying attention to the teacher because he is easily distracted by interesting or stimulating items in and around the classroom. He notices the way that a new mobile hangs and spins in the air. Looking out the window, he is fascinated by a tree moving in the wind. When people enter or leave the classroom, his attention is drawn to the noise and activity by the door. When it's time for free play in the afternoon, one of Brian's favorite things to do is to crash his body repeatedly into the beanbag chair that sits in the reading corner. He has flung himself into it so many times that one of the beanbag's seams has started to rip and its contents are spilling onto the floor.

Brian is a sensory seeker. His nervous system is out of sync because it operates in a nearly continuous state of over-arousal that feels normal to him. As he goes about his day, Brian seeks strong sensory input in just about any way he can get it—through movement, visual stimulation, and tactile pressure. Although his high activity level often seems exhausting to those around him, Brian is wired to be "on the go." Without this additional stimulation, he feels out of sorts and uncomfortable in his own skin, a sensation akin to the experience of wearing an itchy sweater. He therefore continuously looks for ways to stimulate his sensory system to find that "just right" level of comfort (Williamson & Anzalone, 2001). He especially enjoys tactile input and the sensation of deep pressure against his skin, so he likes throwing himself into the beanbag and making physical contact with his peers.

Like Brian, sensory seekers try to find stimuli to fulfill their strong need for sensory input. They might engage in a range of self-stimulating activities such as spinning, running back and forth, jumping, staring at objects, holding objects, and talking or humming to themselves. Sensory-seeking children also tend to have a decreased attention span, and they rapidly shift their focus to stimuli of high interest. Because they so often encounter the world in an over-aroused state, their behavior can seem overbearing, impulsive, and disorganized. These characteristics are evident in the previous example when Brian frequently changes his seating position and, more dramatically, repeatedly crashes his body into the beanbag chair.

STRATEGIES FOR SENSORY SEEKERS

Sensory seekers need assistance in finding appropriate ways to satisfy their high need for stimulation. By giving these children access to sensory input in functional, purposeful ways, we can help them meet their sensory needs without being disorganized and disruptive. In the previous example, Brian's teacher recognizes that repeatedly correcting his behavior is not a productive strategy because he is not willfully breaking the rules; he simply seeks the high level of stimulation that he needs to feel comfortable and focused. She therefore tries to make adjustments to help Brian attain this goal. She puts a bumpy seat cushion on Brian's chair so that he can get sensory input even while sitting down. Sometimes she gives him the opportunity to sit or roll around on a large exercise ball. During circle time or story time, she offers Brian fidgets to hold and squeeze to keep his hands occupied and increase his ability to focus.

The teacher also attempts to set Brian up for success by providing him with opportunities for sensory input well in advance of activities that require quiet and concentration. For example, she might ask him to be her helper in carrying heavy materials from one part of the classroom to another, or she might have him accompany her or another teacher on an errand, giving him the opportunity to walk around and get a change of scenery. If possible, the teacher also tries to give Brian and all the other children time outside to run, climb, and engage in vigorous physical activity before they must do any seated work.

Build Sensory Input into Activities

Even when the weather prevents us from being outside, parents and teachers can make sure to include novel activities that offer sensory seekers like Brian the stimulation they need. Children can make different kinds of "slime," for example; they can find dinosaur fossils in eggs made of ice, or they can build a volcano and make it erupt.

There are also many activities for sensory seekers that require nothing more than a little imagination. For instance, after arranging the chairs in a vertical line and having the children sit down, a "conductor" can take Brian and his peers on a pretend train ride. The teacher shows them how to lean to the side for turns and how to move their bodies up and down when they hit a bump on the tracks. The teacher quickly drags a blanket across the children's heads to simulate a tunnel, and then she blows bubbles to replicate the steam from the engine. As the train gradually comes to the end of its journey, slows down, and pulls into the station, the teacher reestablishes a calm environment in the classroom and helps the children come down from a high level of stimulation. At this point, Brian is likely to be successful in managing the next activity that involves concentrating and sitting still.

Turn Sensory Seekers into Sensory Finders

There are many easy ways to help sensory seekers be successful and feel "just right." We can first make sure to minimize distractions in the environment and to create clear demarcations of space when necessary. We can teach children about personal space "bubbles," and we can reinforce this lesson by having everyone sit on a designated carpet square at circle time. It is also important to provide sensory seekers with the input that their bodies crave. We can weave a range of sensory-based activities seamlessly into a child's day by including opportunities to participate in hands-on play, to engage in physical exercise, and to make use of readily available equipment. These techniques are essential in helping children self-regulate.

Give sensory seekers frequent opportunities for physical movement by implementing the following strategies:

- have them run errands, hand out needed items, and do odd jobs around the classroom or home;
- have them perform gross motor activities by dancing, swinging, rolling, jumping on a mini-trampoline, doing jumping jacks, or playing games like hopscotch; and
- have them engage in heavy work by carrying "heavy" grocery bags, doing crab walks, and doing push-ups against the wall, for example.

Provide sensory seekers with the input they need. Use the following strategies that stimulate the nervous system:

- have them sit on a bumpy cushion or an exercise ball;
- have them wear a backpack or a weighted vest or give them a weighted lap pad, a textured blanket, or a small pillow;
- offer hand fidgets, which can be attached to a child's belt or kept in his pockets for easy access;
- create a sensory corner that includes a water table and sensory bins filled with sand, beans, or rice; and
- offer sensory-rich play activities involving shaving cream, finger painting, Play-Doh, and so forth.

The profiles in this chapter show how sensory processing disorder can be divided into three general classes represented by over-responsiveness, under-responsiveness, and sensory seeking. In each of these cases, children respond differently to the information they take in through their senses.

The over-responsive child perceives sensory input with great acuteness, exhibiting heightened sensitivity to sights, sounds, and touch. Seeking to compensate for a highly reactive nervous system, the over-responsive child often tries to avoid becoming overwhelmed, and as a result, he may rarely show excitement or energetic engagement. The under-responsive child may seem to have a similar disposition but for entirely different reasons. As someone who is less reactive to sensory input, the under-responsive child processes sensory data and environmental stimuli more slowly, which makes it difficult for her to respond effectively to the information she takes in through her senses. She is, consequently, less interactive than her peers, and her state of low arousal produces a flat affect, which may be misinterpreted as boredom or disinterest. Finally, the sensory-seeking child moves through the world in a high state of arousal and needs strong sensory input to feel just right. This child fidgets, moves continually, and is often seen running, jumping, and crashing into things.

In all these cases, the sensory processing difficulties that these children experience compromise their capacity for self-regulation. It is therefore important to implement the strategies that target the challenges that come with each of these sensory profiles. We want to help the over-responsive child avoid becoming overwhelmed, we want to rev up the energy of the under-responsive child, and we want to provide the input that the sensory seeker needs.

Strategies for Different Sensory Profiles		
Over-Responsive Child	*Under-Responsive Child*	*Sensory-Seeking Child*
• Decrease sensory overload • Modify tasks • Preview sensory challenges	• Model active engagement • Increase stimulation • Provide sensory input • Make play enticing	• Build sensory input into everyday activities • Teach about personal space "bubbles" • Offer opportunities for movement and heavy work • Provide fidgets and sensory input for seated work

By creating portraits of these children that are accompanied by relevant strategies, we aim in this chapter to break down the different facets of sensory processing disorder into clear and discrete units. In reality, however, it can be difficult to divide sensory processing issues into such straightforward categories. The next chapter therefore offers general strategies for managing sensory processing disorder. As we shall see, these strategies can be mixed and matched to help children who experience an array of sensory issues that involve both sensory-seeking and sensory-avoidant behavior.

17

GENERAL APPROACHES TO MANAGING SENSORY PROCESSING DISORDER

Because sensory processing issues may not always break down into the discrete classifications described in the previous chapter, it's important to consider more generalized strategies to support children with a range of sensory needs. In daily life, most autistic children exhibit some combination of sensory-seeking and sensory-averse behaviors that interfere with their ability to self-regulate (Williamson & Anzalone, 2001). As parents and teachers, our goal is to take note of the different ways that sensory issues manifest in a child. We then modify the environment and calibrate activities to minimize these sensory challenges and help the child be successful.

If we overwhelm a child's sensory processing abilities or if we fail to provide him with opportunities for the movement and other forms of sensory engagement he needs, we inadvertently set that child up to fail. We should therefore strive to adjust the setting to lessen the demands and difficulties that arise when a child with sensory processing challenges interacts with the world.

Sometimes we try to intervene before fully understanding a child's behavior, but it is important to recognize the clues of sensory processing difficulties so that we can develop effective accommodations. By making modifications to the environment, we can be sensitive to a child's individual challenges and provide support that allows him to feel comfortable, to maintain self-regulation, and to participate in activities along with his peers.

Sensory-related modifications are frequently simple and easy to implement. These adjustments are valuable for helping neurotypical peers, as well, because all children need opportunities both to engage in hands-on activities and to take a break from highly stimulating environments. A sensory-friendly setting is also beneficial to all children because it provides extra support when it comes to developing the key skills of organizing tasks, paying attention, and managing their emotions.

STRATEGIES TO SUPPORT CHILDREN
WITH SENSORY NEEDS

In this section, we review a series of general strategies that are useful for different kinds of sensory processing issues. Some of these techniques involve adjusting the physical environment, whereas others involve planning activities to improve a child's motor skills, coordination, and balance. In addition to focusing on physical space and movement, we also outline helpful practices for enhancing children's coping skills and promoting awareness of how bodily sensations connect to emotions. Finally, we suggest helpful ways that parents and teachers can tailor their interactions with children to ensure that we recognize and respond effectively to a child's sensory needs.

Organize the Physical Space

As we have seen, children with sensory processing issues often have organizational challenges. It is therefore important to arrange the classroom or play area according to function. Set up visual cues regarding what activities are appropriate for each space and include only a reasonable number of toys or other items in each area. Also, clearly designate how many children are allowed in each space at a time. Adding structure and boundaries to the physical environment helps prevent children from feeling overwhelmed and disoriented.

Be Sensitive to the Senses

Consider the subtle ways that ambient noise, lighting, or smells might affect children with sensory processing issues. Avoid using lights that buzz and beware of any noisy machines such as vacuum cleaners or electric hand dryers that might infiltrate the play space. It is difficult for children with sensory processing problems to filter out these extraneous sounds, which interfere with their ability to focus, interact with others, and remain calm. For this reason, it also can be useful to remove any toys that are particularly loud and to remember to play music or videos at reasonable volume levels. If you notice that a child consistently seems bothered by particular sounds, have noise cancelling headphones available for him to wear.

Because many people with sensory processing issues have light sensitivity, allow as much natural light as possible to filter into the classroom or play space. It's ideal if you can avoid using bright fluorescent overhead lights, since these often contribute to sensory overload without people ever being conscious of their effects.

There also may be smells in the environment that can overwhelm children and detract from their ability to focus and participate in the activities at hand. Though many people enjoy the scent of certain cleaning products or the smells of food cooking in the kitchen, this form of sensory input can leave some children feeling nauseated and desperate to escape to fresh air. In these circumstances, it can help to have a "smell eraser" on hand to give a child. There are lots of easy options that can be used for this tool, such as an empty bottle of vanilla extract that still retains its scent or a container of cotton balls that have been dabbed with a citrus-based essential oil.

Make the Break Spot Sensory Friendly

Turn the break spot, as described in chapter 4, into a space where children can go when they need to limit their sensory stimulation. Remember that the break spot is not a time-out place. It should not be associated with any form of punishment. Instead, it is a quiet area that offers children the opportunity to calm down, regroup, and seek solitude. It is ideal if the quiet area can be cordoned off to some degree so that children can feel like they are in a discrete space with some modicum of privacy. We obviously want to make sure that we can still see a child when he is in the quiet area, but we also want to create a cozy space where he can feel protected and removed from the hustle and bustle around him.

Make sure to place soothing items in the quiet space. For example, the space might include beanbags or soft cushions so that children can lie down. It is also useful to provide a weighted blanket or lap pad, accessories offering tactile pressure that some children find comforting. The space might also feature a calming light projector or a special lamp that provides soft, colorful lighting and soothing visual input. There are many sensory-friendly products that can be included in the quiet area to help prompt and reinforce a child's use of important self-calming skills.

Provide Opportunities for Sensory Input

Be sure to include lots of hands-on activities that will fulfill a child's need for a variety of sensory experiences. Having opportunities for messy play gives children the different forms of sensory input that their bodies require; these same opportunities help more reluctant children see that it can be fun to get their hands dirty. Finger paint, shaving cream, rice bins, water tables, and bubble stations are all examples of activities that offer children a range of sensory input. Make sure that children also have plenty of time outside, even on days when the weather is not ideal so that they can have sufficient opportunities for physical activity and ample exposure to fresh air and natural light.

Sometimes children seek sensory input on their own by "stimming," or engaging in repetitive movement that stimulates or calms the nervous system. Such movement might include walking in circles, rocking back and forth, or jumping up and down. It is important to understand the function of self-stimulating behavior and to allow children to engage in it when necessary. Although some people might worry that encouraging children to stim will only increase their atypical behavior, they likely will discover the opposite to be true.

When children have an outlet for stimming, they feel more relaxed, which in turn decreases their need for stimming. It is possible to structure stimming breaks into a child's day as rewards for accomplishing tasks or as a way of enabling him to practice techniques to prevent overstimulation. When a child is stimming, don't assume that he is not listening or that he is disengaged. Self-stimulating activities often help children focus and promote self-regulation.

> **Engaging in self-stimulating activities or "stimming" often helps autistic children focus and promotes self-regulation.**

Improve Motor Skills and Accommodate Deficits

As we have seen, children with sensory processing difficulties often experience delayed development of gross and fine motor skills. These deficits can affect all aspects of a child's participation in an activity as he potentially struggles with understanding the nature of a task, planning the necessary steps to complete the task, and executing the physical movements that the task requires. It's easy to implement fun activities that improve a child's motor planning and gross motor skills. For example, create obstacle courses during outside or inside play by incorporating special but easily manageable equipment. This might include a small balance beam or plastic circles so that children can hop on a path of imaginary lily pads or jump on "rocks" in a pool of hot lava.

Have a special activity where children pretend to crawl like a bear, walk like a crab, hop like a frog, and slither like a snake. All of these movements help strengthen core muscles and improve coordination. Again, practicing and previewing also can be helpful when it comes to sensory issues affecting motor skills. For example, if a child struggles with kicking a ball, practice kicking with the child before the game or ask a peer or parent to practice the skill with the child.

In order to improve fine motor skills, encourage play with items like Play-Doh and help the child roll the dough into a ball, knead it, flatten it into a pancake, cut out shapes, and so forth. It can also be fun to bury small beads or other "treasures" in modeling clay or putty. As the child works to find and pick out the treasure, he practices his pincer grip and develops hand strength.

There are many materials that we can utilize to accommodate children who struggle with fine motor skills so that they feel successful when it comes to art projects, beginning writing, and other similar tasks. Specialized finger grips and crayons that look like rocks are examples of fun tools that also help children eventually learn the correct way to hold a pencil. Drawing letters in shaving cream or pudding is another way for kids to practice early writing and feel successful at the same time. If children struggle with cutting, there are grip loop scissors (without the finger holes) that they can use to build hand strength and get comfortable with the sensation of cutting. The point is to find ways to help children feel successful at activities they might otherwise avoid due to deficits in gross and fine motor skills. By giving children access to inexpensive adaptive equipment and by planning easy yet specialized activities, we enable children to have fun while they are working to improve their motor skills.

There are times, however, when children with sensory processing issues struggle to be successful in motor-based activities, so it is also important that we reinforce the use of coping skills if they get frustrated. Before a game of kickball, for example, remind the child, "If you miss the ball, tell yourself that's just part of the game. Lots of kids miss the ball." If you see the child's frustration quickly mounting, give him the chance to opt out. Ask him if he would like to be the referee or scorekeeper instead.

When a child's participation in an activity is hindered by skill deficits to the point that he feels incompetent and frustrated, insisting that he finish the activity only increases his resistance to trying again in the future. When it comes to motor skill delays, we want to encourage children to take on challenging activities, but we also want them to have positive associations with these activities. Our job is to find ways to increase the likelihood of their being successful and finding enjoyment in tasks that are hard for them because of sensory processing issues.

"Chunk" and Simplify Tasks

Because sensory processing disorder can make it difficult for children to focus and approach a task with a clear plan of action, they might view an activity that we consider to be simple as something that is overwhelming and impossible. Break down difficult tasks into smaller, more reasonable steps so that it seems doable. For example, when teaching a child how to put her coat on, use the well-known "flip" method, which can be broken down into discrete steps. First, show her how to lay her coat on the floor with the tag facing the ceiling. Then show her how to stand with her feet near the tag and help her lean over to put her hands into the sleeves. Finally, aid her in flipping the coat over her head. If the child struggles, focus on mastering one step at a time, working together to complete the whole task. Be there to help and to monitor the child's level of frustration as you go along. Offer the level of support needed for the child to succeed.

Be Consistent

For children with sensory processing problems, the world often feels like a chaotic and overwhelming place. Swinging between phases of over- and under-arousal, these children often experience life as an unpredictable series of extreme emotions and sensory encounters. To combat this sense of disorder, parents and teachers can establish a routine of structured activities. Use a picture schedule to offer children visual cues about what they can expect to happen. When they are familiar with the rhythms of the day, children with sensory processing issues are better prepared to handle the sensations and activities that they find challenging.

For example, if a child is anxious about the weekly music class at her school because she finds it to be too loud, she knows that there is a set, specific time when she must deal with these circumstances—music class is not something to worry about every single day. And by previewing music class, the child and her teacher can develop a plan to help her manage the noise and feel more comfortable. She knows that she can wear headphones or ask to leave the room for a break if she becomes overwhelmed. The sense of predictability and routine helps create a safety net for the difficult situations that the child knows will arise.

Increase Support around Transitions

It may take children with sensory processing disorder more time to finish activities, and they may not be ready to move on to the next scheduled task when they are still working hard to complete a project. They might also be engaged in an activity that feels good to them and find themselves not wanting to transition to another scheduled event that is less appealing from a sensory perspective. For example, a child might be happily working at the puzzle center, enjoying the smell and feel of the wood pieces as he successfully figures out how they click into place. When it's time for him to move on to the dress-up area, however, he refuses to leave the puzzle table because he hates how the dress-up clothes smell and feel and has no interest in putting on scratchy coats and bulky hats, especially since he is already dressed.

In these and other circumstances, it's helpful to use a timer with a visual component so that children know when to expect a change. Give multiple warnings about upcoming transitions so that the child does not feel surprised by having to make a sudden switch to an activity that he has not chosen. It is important to give children with sensory issues additional processing time to consider and prepare for change.

Offer Choices

Giving kids an opportunity to make choices helps them feel more in control, and this feeling is especially important for children with sensory processing issues. Because the environment so powerfully affects these children, influencing their feelings and actions, it is helpful to give them the chance to exert a sense of control. Giving children choices also empowers them to recognize their specific sensory needs. For example, if a child is offered a choice of either finger painting or playing Legos, she can choose the Legos because she knows that she does not like the feeling of finger paint. In this instance she has agency to make a decision that both accommodates her sensory needs and fulfills the teacher's expectation.

In many cases, when children refuse to participate in an activity because of a sensory problem, they feel torn between engaging in a task that feels unappealing or even loathsome to them and disappointing the parent or teacher who expects them to meet a demand. When a child has the opportunity to make a choice that will be accepted, he is empowered to act on his own sensory needs.

Promote Self-Awareness

We can work with children to help them identify their emotions and to connect these feelings to various sensations experienced in the body. The goal is to help children recognize the signs of being over- or under-stimulated and begin to identify the sensory triggers for these feelings. We can encourage children to verbalize how they feel when they are having fun and when they are upset to call explicit attention to the emotions they experience in a given moment.

It is important to highlight instances when they feel "just right," so that they can develop awareness of the good sensations that arise from feeling calm. If a child has had a meltdown that you suspect was caused by a sensory issue, it's important to help the child see that connection for himself after the fact. For example, after a child has had a snack and has fully recovered from an outburst, you might say to him in a friendly, nonjudgmental voice, "I notice that lots of times your body gets angry and upset in the afternoons when it's hungry. Your mouth yells and your hands hit when your stomach is just trying to say that it needs a snack. Let's make sure that you have a little something to eat in the afternoon even if you don't feel hungry. Having some food in your tummy makes it easier for you to calm down if you start to feel angry."

There are also specific programs designed to help children with sensory processing problems develop greater awareness of their emotions in connection with their bodily sensations and actions. One of these, called the Zones of Regulation, associates different colors with different clusters of feelings. Color-coded charts correspond to pictures of facial expressions to help children recognize, for example, that feeling sad, tired, or sick means that they are in the "blue zone"; at the opposite extreme is the "red zone," which includes the emotions of anger, extreme fear, or feeling out of control. (See the appendix for resources on the Zones of Regulation.)

Teach Self-Calming Skills

Because children with sensory processing disorder have difficulty modulating their emotions, it's important to teach concrete techniques that they can use to soothe themselves when they are upset. One effective exercise is deep breathing, and there are many ways to teach children this concept. For example, give them an imaginary cup of hot cocoa and instruct them to breathe the smell in through their nose, then tell them to cool the hot cocoa by blowing out through their mouth.

You also can do another exercise in which you place a small object on the child's stomach while he is lying down on his back. Instruct the child to watch the object move up and down as his stomach rises and falls with the acts of inhaling and exhaling. It can be useful to teach simple yoga positions that promote awareness of the body-mind connection and that help children slow down. A pose that imitates a turtle withdrawing into its shell, for example, offers a concrete image and a plan of action enabling children to use their bodies to withdraw from stressful stimuli when necessary.

There are many resources for teaching child-friendly yoga, including videos and printed cards demonstrating particular poses. We can also teach children that there are calming benefits to very simple acts, such as taking space and engaging in a preferred activity. Help children understand that removing themselves from an upsetting situation is an important coping skill.

Listen Carefully

Children frequently verbalize their needs even if they can't fully articulate the reasons for those needs. For example, after everyone in the class has washed their hands without complaint, one child suddenly refuses to follow suit, getting upset and telling his teacher, "I'm not going to wash my hands. You can't make me do it." In response, the teacher might insist that the child complete this task, explaining to him why it's important to have clean hands. But if the child is struggling to cope with an overreactive response to sensory stimuli, he is unlikely to be persuaded by logical explanations, and it is quite possible that he only will grow more agitated and resistant to the task at hand.

In this case, it's best to look for a workable alternative—something that does not provoke the same strong sensory reaction. Try filling the sink with bubbles that the child can "play" in for a few minutes or perhaps offer him hand sanitizer or wet wipes to use. The point is that we need to listen carefully to a child's words and trust what he says to indicate his needs even if—and especially if—he shows resistance to a particular task or activity. Remember that if a child could wash his hands without any problem, he would fulfill that demand just like all of his peers; however, his sensory perceptions have gone awry, making a simple task feel impossible and overwhelming to him.

If a child shows signs of distress or other extreme emotion as he tells us, "This is too hard" or "I can't do this," we need to respect his efforts at communicating his needs. *Do not insist that a child participate in or complete a task when he clearly tells you that he is not able to do it.* Allow the child to express his feelings and let him know that you have heard and understood his words. Offer him choices, give him the opportunity to take space or to have some time to himself, and use chunking, when appropriate, to break complex tasks into manageable steps.

Be Sensitive to Emotional Reactions

Sensory processing challenges can produce strong emotional reactions in children. Feelings of annoyance and anxiety that often go unnoticed by adults can build in children throughout the course of the day, culminating in an episode of extreme sadness, anger, or fear. It sometimes can be hard to see the link between a seemingly minor event or experience and a child's big emotional reaction. For example, at lunchtime the teacher asks a child to throw away a piece of foil that she left on the table. The child first pretends not to hear and heads to another part of the classroom. When the teacher reminds her of the expectation that everyone needs to throw their trash away, the child starts crying and attempts to run out of the classroom. The teacher brings her back and asks what is wrong, and the child continues sobbing and says, "You are so mean. How could you make me touch that disgusting thing? I have to get out of here."

Be prepared for emotional responses that do not necessarily seem commensurate with the demands of a given situation. When confronted with a child's strong outbursts of feeling, be sure to react in a calm manner and ask, "What's up?" giving the child an opportunity to express her concerns. Often we can help children calm down quickly just by listening and validating their feelings, enabling them to see that they are capable of completing a task that seemed impossible only moments before. However, if they remain unable to handle the task even after they are calm, we can help them by modeling problem-solving skills.

Returning to the previous example, we could show the child a method of throwing the foil away without having to touch it, or we could show the child how to ask for help and communicate her feelings. By giving children an opportunity to express their concerns and by listening to their perspectives, we often can uncover the reasons for a particular behavior and help them work through the problem.

This chapter offers many practical techniques to help children manage sensory processing challenges, but perhaps the most important strategy involves expanding and changing our mind-set as parents and teachers. When we encounter a child having difficulty, it's important to be open to the possibility that sensory issues may be the source of the problem. If a child shows noncompliant behavior, extreme emotion, or complete withdrawal, often the best response is not to react instantaneously but to consider how the child's surface action (or inaction) might be a sign of something deeper rooted in sensory processing difficulties. These difficulties, as we have seen, manifest themselves in highly varied ways impacting everything from a child's cognitive performance and

> **Given that sensory processing disorder has such a broad range of effects, we must guard against the impulse to see behavioral difficulties simply as the result of a child's bad choices.**

motor skills to social and emotional fluency—areas that all, in turn, affect the capacity for self-regulation. Given that sensory processing disorder has such a broad range of effects, we must guard against the impulse to see behavioral difficulties simply as the result of a child's bad choices.

Rather, we should strive to be sensitive and flexible in our interactions with autistic children. Instead of expecting the child to change and adapt to our demands, we must change our demands to adapt to the child's needs. By modifying the environment, simplifying tasks, or even simply listening to a child's words, we can promote self-regulation and provide a sense of much-needed security to children who often find the world to be an unpredictable and overwhelming place.

THE TAKEAWAY

Sensory processing disorder affects many children with autism, often causing them to struggle profoundly with self-regulation. Autistic children can swing between increased and lowered states of arousal—sometimes being averse to sight, sound, and touch and sometimes seeking out such sensations. In addition to affecting the five major senses, the disorder also impacts the vestibular, proprioceptive, and interoceptive systems, which control balance, spatial awareness, and recognition of internal sensations such as hunger or tiredness. Because the eight senses govern so many of our actions in the world, people struggle in many different arenas when they experience sensory processing challenges.

As we have shown, sensory processing disorder can have physical manifestations, causing impairments in motor skills, coordination, and core muscle strength. The disorder can also have cognitive and emotional effects. Some children, for example, need extra time to process information taken in through the senses, whether that information is conveyed visually or verbally. Children with sensory processing challenges also often have difficulty with transitions, and they can become easily frustrated and struggle to regulate their mood.

Given that sensory issues influence so many areas of human functioning, it can be helpful, as we have seen, to gain a basic understanding of sensory processing disorder by focusing on its three dominant sensory profiles: over-responsive, under-responsive, and sensory-seeking children. Each of these encompasses a range of distinctive responses to input perceived through the senses. For each classification, there is a coherent set of strategies that parents and teachers can use to help children feel "just right." These strategies might involve providing children with the sensory input they need or with minimizing sensory input to prevent them from becoming overwhelmed.

In addition to targeting the major types of sensory processing disorder, it is also helpful to employ more general strategies that are applicable to the different combinations of challenges that we often see in children whose sensory needs don't necessarily fit neatly into a single category. After taking the time to investigate the individual nature of a child's sensory issues, we can make a number of easy interventions to ease the challenges he faces and promote his self-regulation.

For example, we can focus on the physical space, making adjustments to the environment when lights, noise, smells, or clutter seem to interfere with a child's daily functioning. We can make sure to incorporate into the daily schedule activities that enhance children's gross motor skills, fine motor skills, and core muscle strength. For example, we can have children navigate simple obstacle courses, draw letters in shaving cream, or walk like different animals. In addition to maintaining a consistent schedule and increasing support around transitions, we can also use different programs and activities to promote self-awareness in children so that they can begin to recognize the signs of feeling over- or under-stimulated. We eventually want them to be able to identify the sensory triggers for such feelings and to turn to the self-calming skills we've taught them to get back into the "just right" zone.

Finally, we want to stress the importance of listening to children and taking seriously their efforts at communicating their sensory needs even if they aren't yet able to articulate those needs clearly. Sensory processing issues often lie at the root of a child's difficulties with certain tasks or demands, and it is likely that their previous experiences with sensory challenges have left a big impression on them. As sensory thinkers, they tend to form memories and experience strong emotions in reaction to sensory stimuli.

We want to support children in learning to recognize and manage the sensory experiences that sometimes overwhelm them. We must therefore listen to their words and find simple alternatives for activities that outstrip their sensory processing resources. If they show signs of becoming completely overwhelmed, we should also offer them a break, recognizing that if the child could complete the task without falling apart, he would do just that. Approaching a child's sensory needs from a place of support and understanding helps him get through a difficult moment and, more importantly, shows him that there are techniques and accommodations we can use to manage sensory challenges and stay in control. When we prioritize self-regulation, we ultimately help the child recognize that he has tools for coping with even the most uncomfortable feelings and sensations he experiences.

CONCLUSION

A New Lens of Understanding

This book aims to increase our understanding of young children with autism so that we can set them up for success. In addition to highlighting the strengths of these children, we've also offered a new lens into their struggles, explaining how the foundational skill of self-regulation is impacted by the different challenges associated with autism. When autistic children exhibit behavior that's labeled "difficult," "extreme," or "unusual," their actions are rooted in neurological differences that affect their social skills, emotional awareness, and sensory processing abilities. We've emphasized that it is critical for parents and teachers to understand the perspectives of autistic children, and we have suggested practical strategies to help them thrive.

Autistic children are doing the best they can. They want to self-regulate—that is, to control themselves and their emotions—but they frequently are overwhelmed by challenges with communication, social interaction, and sensory processing. It requires a great deal of effort for children with autism to find ways to comfort themselves and reduce their anxiety. By teaching them self-regulation, we can help these children manage their strong feelings and interact with people effectively.

As parents and teachers, we must approach autistic children with an attitude of collaboration and understanding. By making small yet meaningful adjustments to their environment, we can facilitate their learning and capacity for self-management. For example, we can increase structure and predictability by previewing upcoming events and using visual schedules.

When autistic children seek to manage challenging situations and troubling feelings, they can be quite resourceful, avoiding tasks that increase their confusion and anxiety or trying novel ways to complete tasks. If we view their actions through our new lens of understanding, we can see that

161

these children are not being oppositional or noncompliant; rather, they are coping with different challenges the best way they know how. When we offer strategies for children to feel safe, secure, and in control of themselves, we greatly improve a child's ability to participate in activities and engage with other people. *We must remember that without self-regulation, a child is unable to follow directions, interact effectively with others, or feel comfortable in his own skin.*

A key way to help autistic children develop the foundational skill of self-regulation is to offer support in the specific areas that prove challenging for them. When it comes to communicating their emotional needs, for example, it's clear that autistic children want to be heard, but they may not know how to express themselves even if they are highly articulate. Such children often have important information to share but may feel overwhelmed or confused. They may shut down, isolate themselves, or seek attention in ineffective or off-putting ways. As parents and teachers, we should strive to be patient, allow extra time for children to express themselves, and ask simple questions like, "What's up?" in order to gain insight into their perspective. When autistic children are distressed, we need to offer them encouragement to calm down, take a break, and regroup.

Many people assume that autistic children are happier on their own, but they frequently want to engage and play with others. They are unsure about how to make friends and navigate the unwritten rules of the social world. We can offer these children helpful strategies to deal with unpredictable and daunting social situations. By explicitly teaching social skills and implementing techniques that increase social thinking, we can help autistic children develop a tool kit that gives them a solid foundation for successfully interacting with others and building friendships.

Even in their everyday environments, children on the autism spectrum can feel overwhelmed by ordinary sensations, or they may seek the extra sensory input that their bodies need. Autistic children work hard to understand and interpret the information they take in through their senses—information that is often confusing and hard to differentiate among a barrage of different sensations. With the knowledge that autistic children have distinctive sensory needs, we can plan activities and give children tools to help them feel "just right."

It is important, finally, to acknowledge that children on the autism spectrum are not inferior to neurotypical children. Their brains are wired differently, and many strengths come with their unique experience of the world. For example, autistic children can be excellent problem solvers; their prodigious memories and great attention to detail are traits that will serve them well in many facets of life. It should also go without saying that autistic children, just like neurotypical children, can be loving, funny, helpful, polite, and intelligent—to name only a few positive attributes. We don't want autistic children to lose the qualities that make them special and unique, but we do want them to feel more secure in a world that can seem unpredictable and overwhelming.

Our hope is that parents and teachers use this book to build on the many strengths of autistic children so as to draw a road map for promoting self-regulation, social interaction, play skills, and sensory integration. By providing reinforcement and using the supportive strategies we outline, parents and teachers can lay the groundwork for children to have successful futures as engaged, fulfilled, and self-confident adults.

APPENDIX

GENERAL RESOURCES

- Autism Spectrum Disorder Fact Sheet, the National Institute of Neurological Disorders and Stroke: www.ninds.nih.gov/Disorders/Patient-Caregiver-Education/Fact-Sheets/Autism-Spectrum-Disorder-Fact-Sheet
- Floortime, the Interdisciplinary Council on Development and Learning: www.icdl.com
- The Star Institute for Sensory Processing Disorder: www.spdstar.org/basic/about-spd
- Social Thinking: www.socialthinking.com

STRATEGIES AND TOOLS

- Visual schedules: www.iidc.indiana.edu/pages/using-visual-schedules-a-guide-for-parents
- Behavior charts (reward charts for behavior modification): www.freeprintablebehaviorcharts.com
- The Incredible 5 Point Scale: www.autismempowerment.org/wp-content/uploads/2013/12/Incredible-5-Point-Scale-Fact-Sheet-rev.pdf
- Social stories: carolgraysocialstories.com
- Feelings poster, "How Do You Feel Today?": www.childswork.com/collections/posters
- Feelings thermometer: https://copingskillsforkids.com/blog/2016/4/27/making-a-feelings-thermometer

- Zones of Regulation: www.zonesofregulation.com
- Child friendly yoga: www.kidsyogastories.com/kids-yoga-poses/
- Howda chair: www.howdachair.com

BOOKS

- *Preschool SENSE: Sensory Scan for Educators*, by Carol S. Kranowitz (Las Vegas, NV: Sensory Resources, 2005).
- *The Kids' Guide to Staying Awesome and in Control: Simple Stuff to Help Children Regulate Their Emotions and Senses*, by Lauren Brukner (London: Jessica Kingsley, 2014).
- *Comic Strip Conversations: Illustrated Interactions That Teach Conversation Skills to Students with Autism and Related Disorders*, by Carol Gray (Arlington, TX: Future Horizons, 1994).
- *When My Worries Get Too Big: A Relaxation Book for Children Who Live with Anxiety*, by Kari Dunn Buron (Shawnee Mission, KS: AAPC, 2013).
- *Kids in the Syndrome Mix of ADHD, LD, Autism Spectrum, Tourette's, Anxiety, and More! The One-Stop Guide for Parents, Teachers, and Other Professionals* (2nd ed.), by Martin L. Kutscher (London: Kingsley, 2014).
- *A Practical Guide to Autism: What Every Parent, Family Member, and Teacher Needs to Know*, by Fred R. Volkmar and Lisa A. Wiesner (Hoboken, NJ: Wiley, 2009).

REFERENCES

Asperger, H. (1991). "Autistic psychopathy" in childhood (U. Frith, Trans.). In U. Frith (Ed.), *Autism and Asperger syndrome* (pp. 37–92). New York: Cambridge University Press. (Original work published 1944).

Attwood, T. (2007). *The complete guide to Asperger's syndrome.* London: Jessica Kingsley.

Baron-Cohen, S. (2001). Theory of mind in normal development and autism. *Prisme 34,* 174–83.

Buron, K. D. (2012). *The incredible five-point scale.* Shawnee Mission, Kansas: AAPC.

Campbell, S. B. (2006). *Behavior problems in preschool children: Clinical and developmental issues.* 2nd ed. New York: Guilford Press.

Charman, T., et al. (1997). Infants with autism: an investigation of empathy, pretend play, joint attention, and imitation. *Developmental Psychology 35*(5), 781–89.

Cheng, W., et al. (2015). Autism: Reduced connectivity between cortical areas involved in face expression, theory of mind, and the sense of self. *Brain 138*(5), 1382–93. doi:10.1093/brain/awv051

Civil Rights Data Collection. (2013–2014). Retrieved from www2.ed.gov/about/offices/list/ocr/docs/crdc-2013-14.html

Coplan, J. (2010). *Making sense of autism spectrum disorders.* New York: Bantam.

Dapretto M., et al. (2006). Understanding emotions in others: Mirror neuron dysfunction in children with autism spectrum disorders. *Nature Neuroscience 9*(1), 28–30.

Fiene, L., & Brownlow, C. (2015). Investigating interoception and body awareness in adults with and without autism spectrum disorder. *Autism Research 8*(6), 708–16. doi:10.1002/aur.1486

Frith, U., & de Vignemont, F. (2005). Egocentrism, allocentrism, and Asperger syndrome. *Consciousness and Cognition 14,* 719–38.

Frith, U., & Frith, C. (2009). The social brain: Allowing humans to boldly go where no other species has been. *Philosophical Transactions of the Royal Society B, 24,* 165–76.

Garfinkel, S. N., et al. (2016). Discrepancies between dimensions of interoception in autism: Implications for emotion and anxiety. *Biological Psychology 114*, 117–26. doi:10.1016/j.biopsycho.2015.12.003

Gilliam, W. S. (2005). Prekindergarteners left behind: Expulsion rates in state prekindergarten systems. Yale University Child Study Center, 1–13.

Gopnik, A. (2016). *The gardener and the carpenter: What the new science of child development tells us about the relationship between parents and children.* New York: Farrar, Straus and Giroux.

Grandin, T. (1995). *Thinking in pictures.* New York: Random House.

Grandin, T. (2013). *The autistic brain.* New York: Houghton Mifflin Harcourt.

Greene, R. W. (2014a). *The explosive child.* New York: Harper.

Greene, R. W. (2014b). *Lost at school.* New York: Scribner.

Greenspan, S., & Wieder, S. (1998). *The child with special needs.* Boston: Merloyd Lawrence.

Hua, X., et al. (2011). Brain growth rate abnormalities visualized in adolescents with autism. *Human Brain Mapping 20.* doi:10.1002/hbm.21441

Isbell, C., & Isbell, R. (2007). *Sensory integration: A guide for preschool teachers.* Beltsville, MD: Gryphon.

Jaswal, V., & Akhtar, N. (2018). Being vs. appearing socially uninterested: Challenging assumptions about social motivation in autism. *Behavioral and Brain Sciences*, 1–84. doi:10.1017/S0140525X18001826

Jones, A. P., et al. (2010). Feeling, caring, knowing: Different types of empathy deficit in boys with psychopathic tendencies and autism spectrum disorder. *Journal of Child Psychology and Psychiatry 51*(11), 1188–97.

Kaufman, R. (2014). *Autism breakthrough: The groundbreaking method that has helped families all over the world.* New York: St. Martin's Griffin.

Koegel, R., & Koegel, L. (1995). *Teaching children with autism.* Baltimore: Paul H. Brookes.

Kranowitz, C. (2003). *The out-of-sync child has fun.* New York: Penguin.

Kranowitz, C. (2005). *The out-of-sync child.* New York: Penguin.

Leslie, K. R, et al. (2004). Functional imaging of face and hand imitation: Towards a motor theory of empathy. *Neuroimage 21*(2), 601–7.

Nason, B. (2014). *The autism discussion page on the core challenges of autism: A toolbox for helping children with autism feel safe, accepted, and competent.* London: Jessica Kingsley.

Oberman, L. M., & Ramachandran, V. S. (2007). The simulating social mind: The role of the mirror neuron system and simulation in the social and communicative deficits of autism spectrum disorders. *Psychological Bulletin 133*(2), 310–27.

Prizant, B. M. (2015). *Uniquely human: A different way of seeing autism.* New York: Simon & Schuster.

Quill, K. (2000). *Do-watch-listen-say: Social communication intervention for children with autism.* Baltimore: Paul H. Brookes.

Reebye, P., & Stalker, A. (2010). *Understanding regulation disorders of sensory processing in children.* London: Jessica Kingsley.

Rutishauser, U., et al. (2013). Single-neuron correlates of atypical face processing in autism. *Neuron 80*, 887–99.

Shannon, J. B. (Ed.). (2011). *Autism and pervasive developmental disorders sourcebook.* Detroit, MI: Omnigraphics.

Stillman, W. (2002). *Demystifying the autistic experience: A humanistic introduction for parents, caregivers and educators.* London: Jessica Kingsley.

Stillman, W. (2010). *The everything parent's guide to children with Asperger's syndrome: The sound advice and reliable answers you need to help your child succeed.* Avon, MA: Adams Media.

Stoddart, K. (2005). *Children, youth and adults with Asperger syndrome: Integrating multiple perspectives.* London: Jessica Kingsley.

Suskind, R. (2014). *Life animated: A story of sidekicks, heroes, and autism.* Los Angeles: Kingswell.

Szatmari, P. (2004). *A mind apart: Understanding children with autism and Asperger syndrome.* New York: Guilford Press.

Williamson, G., & Anzalone, M. (2001). *Sensory integration and self-regulation in infants and toddlers: Helping very young children interact with their environment.* Washington, DC: Zero to Three. National Center for Infants, Toddlers, and Families.

Winner, Michelle Garcia. (2007). *Thinking about you thinking about me.* Santa Clara, CA: Think Social Publishing.

Yi Shin, C., et al. (2016). White matter microstructure is associated with auditory and tactile processing in children with and without sensory processing disorder. *Frontiers in Neuroanatomy 9.* doi:10.3389/fnana.2015.00169

ABOUT THE AUTHORS

Dr. **Karin Donahue** is an assistant professor of psychology at Northampton Community College in Bethlehem, Pennsylvania, and a behavior specialist consultant specializing in autism. She has more than thirty years of clinical experience working with children and their families. Dr. Donahue is the mother of two grown children and lives in Quakertown, Pennsylvania, with her husband and two dogs.

Dr. **Kate Crassons** is an associate professor of English at Lehigh University and the director of Lehigh University Press. Her research and teaching focus on a range of topics including social justice, neurodiversity, and disability studies. She lives in Bethlehem, Pennsylvania, with her husband and two sons. Crassons is also the author of *The Claims of Poverty: Literature, Culture, and Ideology in Late Medieval England* (2010).